CRUSH YOUR LIMITS

BREAK FREE FROM LIMITATIONS AND
ACHIEVE YOUR TRUE POTENTIAL

THIBAUT MEURISSE

CONTENTS

Who is This Book For?

You'll greatly benefit from this book if you want to:

- Stop feeling stuck where you are now and turn your life around
- Transform your vision of yourself and the world by adopting powerful beliefs that will earn you remarkable results
- Discover how much more potential you have and start tapping into your greatness
- Program your subconscious to reach higher levels of success, and
- Overcome mental blocks such as feelings of worthlessness and money-related fears and move freely towards your goals.

What You'll Discover in This Book

In this book, you will:

- Learn how much you've been limiting yourself, and be challenged to expand your thinking to grow more than you thought possible
- Uncover disempowering assumptions that have been sabotaging your success and undermining your happiness and peace of mind for years
- Learn how to replace limiting beliefs with more empowering ones to help you move freely towards your goals and dreams, and
- Be challenged to redefine your relationships with key concepts such as time, money, work and success, which

will leave you with a whole new perspective and will inspire you to take massive action.

How to Use This Book

I encourage you to read all the way through this book at least once. After that, I invite you to revisit the book and focus on the section(s) you want to explore in more depth. As you'll learn here, repetition is key. Don't hesitate to read this book multiple times.

You'll find many exercises in this book. Most of them are simple and don't require much time, so make sure you do them.

Also, I highly encourage you to join the 30-Day Challenge, which will help you start reprogramming your mind and create a powerful mindset that will serve you for the rest of your life.

If you feel this book could be of any use to your family members or friends, make sure to share it with them.

YOUR FREE ACTION GUIDE

To help you overcome your limitations I've created a **free action guide**. Make sure you download it at the URL below or use the action guide available at the end of this book.

http://whatispersonaldevelopment.org/crush-limits

FOREWORD BY MIKE PETTIGREW

Limiting beliefs are one of the biggest reasons people fail to achieve their goals and fail to attain a better quality of life.

Everyone has limiting beliefs, and they sabotage your chances of success. Sadly, most people are blissfully unaware of their own limiting beliefs, even though they enact a powerful influence over their lives.

Many years ago, I became acutely aware of my own limiting beliefs surrounding money, at a time when I was experiencing a financial rollercoaster.

Three years earlier, I started my first real business, which was going quite well except for the fact that I was constantly experiencing financial difficulties. It was literally, feast or famine. One month there was plenty of money, while the next there was barely enough cash for me to eat properly. At that point, I had no idea the root source of my money problems lay in my low self-worth.

As a child, I suffered from asthma, and I couldn't run very far. My classmates soon discovered I was useless at sports and that I was the worst player to be on their sports team. They used to argue over not having me on their team. They would say things like, "We don't want Pettigrew, we had him last week and he's useless."

Most of our beliefs are formed through repetition and emotion, and when you hear you are useless again and again, you can start to believe it, just like I did.

As Henry Ford, creator of the first automobiles used to say, "Whether you think you can, or you think you can't – you're right." What we believe becomes our reality. If we think we can't achieve something, no matter how hard we may try, our beliefs will sabotage that goal.

Right through my teens and into my early twenties I thought I was useless at all sorts of things and, because I thought I was useless, I *was* incompetent and clumsy.

This became a vicious circle and, no matter how hard I tried to improve my finances, I still continued to experience money problems. Then I hit a brick wall—a problem so big I thought I was going to have to fold up the business.

I discovered that I owed our suppliers more money that month than was coming in during the following two months. I was deeply shocked, and I had no idea what to do. I considered all sorts of strategies but could not envisage any of them working.

I almost decided to close the business and work for someone else when it dawned on me, if I ceased trading, I would have wasted four years of very hard work—and all for nothing.

Around the same time, I experienced other events that showed me I had low self-worth. I started thinking about those experiences and wondered whether my money problems could also be related to my poor self-value.

As a last-ditch attempt to rescue my business and livelihood and to boost my self-worth, I doubled my prices. Even if half my clients stop doing business with me, my business would have still been in a far better position financially.

So, I wrote to each of my clients, explaining that if they wished to continue receiving the same level of service they had come to expect from my business, we would have to increase our prices dramatically.

Amazingly, every single one of them agreed to the 100% price increase, and one of them even told me that he had always thought that I was charging far too little anyway!

From that point forward my business start to thrive and become seriously profitable. So much so that a few years later, I sold the first business to a multinational, and by that point, I was a millionaire with lots of self-value!

Everything changed as soon as I started rooting out and overcoming my limiting beliefs.

Your limiting beliefs are among the biggest obstacles you face in your life. They hold you back enormously and stop you from achieving success, happiness, freedom and wealth. You may think you have no limiting beliefs, or that limiting beliefs don't hold you back from achieving your dreams, but you are mistaken.

From the moment you were born, you have been conditioned to believe certain things that are simply not true. You have been "told" by your parents, siblings, friends, and teachers how you should think, feel, react and behave. You have also been conditioned to believe you can only achieve certain things, and that certain aspirations are too unrealistic and impossible for you.

Then, as you move through life, you experience difficulties and setbacks that compound the problem. By the time most people reach the age of thirty, they have experienced so much conditioning and so many painful experiences their realm of possibility has been dramatically reduced.

How many people give up on the dreams they had as a child, a teenager or while in their early twenties? It is a sad reality, but most adults end up settling for a dissatisfying mediocrity—for the rest of their lives!

But what if there were a different way? What if it were possible to dramatically reduce the stream of negative thoughts and limiting beliefs that go through our minds continuously?

Imagine what it would be like if you were able to switch off those limiting beliefs. What might start happening in your life? Many people have found the secret that allows them to do this, and their lives have changed in miraculous ways as a result.

When you overcome your limiting beliefs, what once seemed impossible suddenly becomes possible. You wipe the slate clean and you can start again. It does not matter how many failures and setbacks you have experienced in the past. The fact is, you can recreate yourself every single day of your life—providing you choose to do so.

Then again, you can continue to live your present and future life based on your past failures, thereby locking yourself into a restrictive and disempowering future. The choice is yours.

I have discovered from abundant personal experience over many years that the greatest secret to success lies in the ability to root out and overcome our limiting beliefs. This may seem difficult, or even impossible to do, but it is a lot easier than you may currently believe.

Thibaut Meurisse has created a vitally important book on overcoming your limiting beliefs, and I applaud him for creating this masterpiece. In the pages of this groundbreaking book you will learn the easy way to overcome all your limiting beliefs, so you can finally create the life you truly yearn for.

I absolutely love this book, and I am so excited that Thibaut has written it. This is because I know it will help millions of people around the world to transform their lives and become happy and deeply fulfilled.

You really *can* wipe the slate clean. You absolutely *can* start again. You definitely *can* create the life you were born to live! And you can do all this more quickly than you may have ever dreamed possible.

Read this book through once, so you get a good understanding of how it works and what you can gain by using it. Then go back to the sections that apply most to you. Pick out the limiting beliefs holding you back in any area of your life and follow the simple steps Thibaut shares with you.

This book is one-of-a-kind, and it can totally change your life. You are holding in your hands the key to achieving the life that you yearn for. Expect massive transformations from this point forwards!

Very best wishes,

Mike Pettigrew

Serial entrepreneur and author of the bestseller, *The Most Powerful Goal Achievement System in the World.*

INTRODUCTION

If you put a chain around the leg of an elephant when it is still young, initially, it will try to escape. However, unable to do so, it will eventually give up and stop resisting. As it grows bigger and stronger, it could easily break free, but it never will. Instead, it will remain under the control of its trainer for the rest of its life. Why? Because it has been conditioned to believe it can't escape.

What if the only thing preventing you from living the life you want is the illusion that you can't? What if the reasons you're not where you want to be is the result of similar conditioning to that of the elephant? What if this conditioning is the result of the many assumptions you hold in various areas of your life?

Now, imagine if you could transform your life simply by changing these assumptions. Could you be a few *new* assumptions away from success and happiness?

The truth is you're operating far below your maximum capabilities. In fact, we all are. Your current assumptions lead you to think, feel and act in a way that is incongruent with the results you want to obtain and the person you want to become.

I believe it is possible for you to experience more happiness, success and fulfillment than you can ever imagine. How? By reframing your life, by questioning the way you think, feel and act, and by replacing your current limiting assumptions with more empowering ones.

This book will help you reframe your life to unlock the whole of your potential. With this book, I want you to expand your horizons and fully realize the field of possibilities ahead of you. Throughout this book, we will work on loosening and reforming your assumptions, and we will remove unsupportive assumptions. On many occasions, I will challenge the beliefs you hold in various areas of your life. You may not agree with everything I say. Occasionally, you may even become defensive or angry, and that's fine. What matters most is that you start questioning all your limiting assumptions.

As you read this book, I will ask you to be proactive. Nothing works until you do. And only you can do the work. This is *your* life. Work it. Improve it. Win!

Here is a more detailed summary of what you'll learn in this book:

In **Part I**, we will define assumptions and discuss how they limit you. You'll learn how your assumptions have been affecting your life more than you probably think.

In **Part II**, we will review fifty common assumptions that may be preventing you from reaching your full potential. We'll discuss the assumptions you hold about yourself, life, success, emotions, work and time.

Finally, in **Part III**, we will learn how you can replace your disempowering assumptions with more empowering ones, so you can make positive changes in your life and achieve your goals and dreams.

PART I

UNDERSTANDING ASSUMPTIONS

1

EACH ASSUMPTION YOU HOLD LIMITS YOU

Right now, you hold thousands of assumptions that limit your field of possibilities. While some assumptions bear little to no significant consequences, others impact your entire life. Some examples of major assumptions include: "I can't be happy because of X, Y or Z," or "I can't ask for what I want." These two assumptions alone can limit you dramatically and prevent you from designing and living the life you want. And these are just the tip of the iceberg.

A minor assumption could be something as simple as, "I should always answer the phone," or "I should avoid blanks in the conversation."

Your assumptions—minor or major—determine the choices available to you in any situation. They are the rules you add to the game of life which often make it more challenging than it needs to be.

My hope is that, while reading and working through this book, you'll realize how much you've been limiting yourself, and you'll be able to start unlocking the unlimited potential within you.

Are you really stuck?

Perhaps you feel stuck right now. You may have been in a dead-end job or in an unfulfilling relationship for years. Perhaps you have not been making enough progress in your career or your business. Perhaps, you've been struggling to lose weight for as long as you can remember.

If you're feeling stuck, it's mostly the result of the way your mind works. Your mind operates within a certain set of rules. These rules are what I call "assumptions." These same assumptions determine the way you interpret your thoughts and the events around you and, as a result, the actions you take. Therefore, to obtain different (and better) results, you must challenge your assumptions. The first step is to assess whether they are true and whether they are limiting or empowering you.

Are you really stuck? Or is your situation determined by one of these assumptions? If so, ask yourself, if I knew what to do, would I do it? What can I do to improve my situation?

Sadly, many people believe they have no power to transform their lives. I firmly believe this couldn't be further from the truth. In fact, the way you currently think, feel and act is only a tiny fraction of the almost infinite possibilities available to you. It probably doesn't even represent 0.1% of the thoughts you could have, the feelings you could experience or the actions you could take.

In what way are you limiting yourself right now? What disempowering story are you telling yourself? What options haven't you reflected on yet?

Consider the following: every single day we have thousands of thoughts—some research suggests fifty thousand or more—and make over thirty-five thousand decisions. How much power do you think you can harness once you start changing some of your thoughts for the better? How fast do you think you can change your life once you start making a few different (and better) decisions each day? The same way an airplane can land in a totally different place if it slightly deviates from its course, a human being will end up in a totally different position if he or she changes a few dominant thoughts or habits.

In my experience, simply adopting a few new, and positive, daily habits can lead to dramatic improvements in the long term. Changing two to three daily habits is usually all it takes to achieve almost any goal, be it becoming an author, losing weight, changing career or earning a promotion. Even simple habits like avoiding hitting the snooze button or taking a few minutes to set goals every day can dramatically impact your life long-term. You certainly don't lack opportunities to change, you merely lack perspective.

2

HOW YOUR ASSUMPTIONS AFFECT YOUR LIFE

For years, I've been fascinated by the effect assumptions can have on people's lives. Simply assuming you can't do something means you'll probably never be able to do it. Or, as Henry Ford once said, *"Whether you think you can or think you can't—you're right."*

In reality, you *can* do most of the things you believe you can't—even if you're convinced of the opposite.

In his book, *The Success Principles,* Jack Canfield relates the story of Victor Serebriakoff, the son of a Russian émigré who grew up in a London slum. His story illustrates well how an individual's assumptions can affect their whole life. Victor's teachers labeled him a dunce and encouraged him to drop out of school. Victor believed his teachers and became an itinerant worker. He was often forced to live on the streets and had lost any hope to ever live a "normal" life.

At age thirty-two, he joined the British army. The intelligence test he took revealed he had an IQ of 161. He was a genius! This single number alone changed his destiny. Because he started believing he was smart —as the test said—he acted in a whole different way. After training recruits in the army, he joined a timber company and became a major player in the industry. By inventing a machine for grading timber and through holding several patents, he even transformed the timber industry. Later, he was elected chairman of Mensa International, the largest and oldest high IQ society in the world.

Victor's story shows how one false assumption can have major consequences on our lives. We could even argue that if Victor had been lied to—and was in fact of average intelligence—his life would still have changed almost as dramatically.

What about you? What single assumption you currently hold prevents you from living the life you want? What are you convinced you can't do? What if you could actually do that very thing?

Tip:

A great way to shift your perspective is to identify something you believe is impossible and do it. By learning to complete apparently impossible tasks, you'll start shattering your assumptions about what is and isn't feasible and, as a result, open yourself up to a whole new world of opportunity.

What assumptions are

Your assumptions act like filters, coloring your experiences and preventing the light within you from shining. The more filters you add to your lens, the less your light shines and the narrower your field of possibility becomes. In the same way the things in your room don't cease to exist when you turn off the light—you just can't see them in the dark—your potential doesn't suddenly vanish when obstructed by your filters. Your potential has been there all the time, but your self-imposed filters made you blind to it.

Removing your filters means letting go of your assumptions. This doesn't necessarily mean you believe *everything* is possible, but rather that you don't believe or disbelieve anything. For instance, once you have removed your limiting assumptions, when you look at what extraordinary people are doing, you will be able to assume that if they can do it, you can do it as well. You will hold the space for that possibility. In short, you will allow light to penetrate your room rather than obstructing it by holding onto disempowering assumptions.

On the other hand, whenever you add filters, you artificially limit yourself. You start closing the blinds and end up making your room darker than it needs to be. In these circumstances, you believe:

- You're too old (or too young)
- You're not smart or good enough
- You don't know the right people
- You don't have the right education
- You're too shy, or
- You can't do X, Y, Z because it's not "who you are."

In addition, society keeps adding new filters to block even more light. Social pressures define what you're supposed to eat, how you should behave, what you're allowed and not allowed to do.

By the time you're seven, you already operate within a narrow band of possibilities defined by the assumptions you've already adopted unconsciously. As a result, your room is dark and will stay that way. Worse still, it might even become darker as you grow older.

Isn't it time for you to remove these filters and reclaim your power?

Are your assumptions serving you?

Your assumptions can prevent you from unlocking your potential and achieving the life you want. However, some assumptions are better than others and can actually serve you well. In this book, I'll introduce you to powerful assumptions that will greatly expand your field of possibilities and enhance what you can accomplish.

Please note, an assumption doesn't need to be true. In fact, most of your assumptions are false or, at best, only partially true. What matters most is for you to select the assumptions that empower you and allow you to live a more fulfilling life.

A key question to ask yourself is, "Is this particular assumption serving me or working against me? Is it moving me toward my ultimate vision, or is it preventing me from achieving it?" Whenever you come across an assumption that doesn't serve you, replace it with a more empowering one.

What are your specific assumptions?

The way you live your life is ultimately based on major assumptions you hold in various areas of your life. Assumptions are nothing more than ways you relate to different key concepts such as: love, time, money, work, success and emotions.

In short, your entire vision of the world is based on your relationship with concepts and the emotions you attached to them. Just one 'false' assumption—a disempowering way to relate to a key concept—can make your life challenging and create a great deal of suffering.

For example, let's look at the concept of time. Each of us attaches a certain meaning or story to time, which leads us to feel a certain way. You may think you don't have enough time or that time is money and, as a result, you become frustrated when you waste your time. Or perhaps you believe there is no such thing as wasting your time and you savor each moment. Money is another concept to which you may attach all sorts of assumptions, such as money is bad, rich people are greedy or money doesn't grow on trees. Or maybe you think money is great and you want to make as much of it as you possibly can.

The assumptions we hold for all the concepts stored in our minds determines how we think, feel and act, as well as how we perceive the world. While we tend to assume that other people see the world more or less the same way we do, that is certainly not the case. There are as many worldviews as there are people living on this planet.

In this section, we'll look at empowering assumptions about key concepts such as life in general, work, money and time. But before we delve into that, I would like you to reflect on your own relationship with these major assumptions. Bear in mind that how you currently see yourself, money, time and any other concept, is based on the assumptions you hold, and this is just one possible interpretation.

To make the most of this book, keep an open mind and be ready to challenge your deepest beliefs whenever necessary.

Take a few minutes to do the following exercise before you read further. This is the foundation for the work we'll do together throughout this book, and it will allow you to pinpoint areas in which you can adopt more empowering assumptions to make a positive difference in your life.

Exercise:

Complete the following sentences with whatever comes to your mind. Write as many answers as you like.

- Life is ...
- Success is ...
- Emotions are ...
- I am ...
- Money is ...
- Time is ...
- Work is ...

Now you have uncovered some of your assumptions, let's have a look at some major assumptions that may be limiting your success.

PART II

UNCOVERING COMMON ASSUMPTIONS

In this section, we'll investigate fifty common assumptions. We'll cover the following topics: life in general, success, money, emotions, work and time. For each assumption there will be a simple exercise. I encourage you to spend a little time to go through it.

In addition, once you finish reading about one assumption, spend a few seconds imagining how that assumption will impact your life if you adopted it.

3

ASSUMPTIONS REGARDING YOUR ASSUMPTIONS

Did you know you have assumptions about your assumptions, or, if you prefer, beliefs about your beliefs? Below are two common assumptions you may have.

Negative assumption #1—I'm convinced of something therefore it must be true

Are you convinced your religious or political beliefs are the correct ones? Guess what? Terrorists are just as convinced as you they're right—if not more so. Your level of certainty regarding your current beliefs is *not* an indicator of their validity. In fact, it's often the opposite.

To start reframing your life and replace disempowering assumptions with more empowering ones, you must realize that your emotional attachment to your current assumptions doesn't make them right.

I encourage you to start challenging your biggest assumptions— the ones that impact your life the most—before moving on to minor ones. Note that your biggest assumptions are often the ones you're the most emotionally attached to.

Here is a new assumption you can adopt instead:

My emotional attachment to a belief doesn't mean it is valid.

Exercise:

Write down your major assumptions. These are the core beliefs you're most strongly attached to. Start opening yourself up to the possibility they may not be true.

Negative assumption #2—My beliefs need to be accurate

You probably want your beliefs to be accurate. If you thought you were wrong, you would choose better ones, wouldn't you?

While striving to hold the most accurate vision possible is great, in truth there are many things you'll never be able to prove. If so, why even have beliefs in the first place?

My answer is: to help you live a better life! That's what this book is all about: adopting empowering assumptions that will allow you to live the best life possible—whether or not these assumptions are true.

For instance:

- Believing God put you on earth to accomplish a specific mission may give you a strong sense of purpose and help you live a better life.
- Believing in life after death may alleviate your fear of death and help you live a more productive, peaceful and joyful life.
- Believing you have the power to achieve any goal may help you achieve more than you otherwise would.

Therefore, rather than holding the assumption that your beliefs must be accurate, why not adopt the following assumption:

I consciously choose to adopt empowering beliefs that transform my life for the better.

Exercise:

Select two or three empowering beliefs that would make the biggest difference in your life, if you were to adopt them.

4

LIFE ASSUMPTIONS

In this section, we'll introduce general assumptions about life.

In the first part, we'll discuss the assumptions you hold about the outside world. That is, the beliefs that the world prevents you from doing what you want to do (e.g. "I'm a victim of my environment.")

In the second part, we'll talk about assumptions you hold about yourself. These are self-imposed limitations, e.g. something is wrong with me, I'm not good enough, etc.

I'm a victim of my environment

Negative assumption #3—Life is hard

Life is hard, isn't it? But what if it isn't? What if life is easy, and you're simply making it harder than it needs to be? Could this be a possibility?

Have you ever thought of the consequences of holding such a negative assumption? Do you think it helps you live a better life? Once your mind believes something, it looks for evidence to prove it. Your mind likes to come up with answers to your questions, and it accepts your assumptions whether they are empowering you or not. Tell your mind "life is hard," and it will come up with reasons to support this assumption. Tell your mind "life is easy," and it will find evidence to support this as well.

Try it now. Ask yourself, why is life so easy?

Start shifting your assumption toward "life is easy." Whenever you find life hard, ask yourself, "How could I be making my life harder than it is? What beliefs do I hold that lead me to struggle more than I need to?"

Perhaps you believe you need something to make you happy and, because you don't have it right now, you are miserable. Maybe all your friends are successful while you see yourself as a "failure." But how do you know they are any happier than you are? What if they have severe issues you don't know about?

Here is a new assumption you can adopt:

Life is easy. And I do whatever I can to keep it this way.

Exercise:

Write down all the reasons why your life is easy. Come up with at least twenty reasons. For instance, life is easy because:

- There is food on the table every day
- I have access to water and electricity
- I have great friends I can meet regularly
- I have access to many incredible services such as the postal service or public transportation

- I have access to great information online for free or at an affordable price.

Negative assumption #4—Others are happier than me

Nowadays, the need to compare ourselves with others is everywhere. Our friends look so happy, especially on Facebook (or so we think). In addition, our email box is full of messages telling us we aren't good enough the way we are. We should make more money, lose weight or be happier.

Believing your friends are happier than you are is a dangerous assumption to hold. How can you know what's going on in their lives? People you envy could be depressed or severely ill and you wouldn't necessarily know it. Even smiles can hide pain. Sometimes a little pain, sometimes tremendous agony. So why assume others have it easier? What you do you have to gain by doing that?

Here is a more empowering assumption:

I'm as happy as anybody else.

Exercise:

Answer the question, "why am I probably as happy as anybody else?" Write down as many answers as you can think of.

Negative assumption #5—I'm the product of my environment

Do you see yourself as a victim? Do you believe you have no power to change your life? If so, you probably assume your social environment determines what you can and cannot do. What if this is not the case? What if your environment isn't the issue here?

What if your environment is the product of *you* and, as you change, your environment will change also?

Sadly, most people tend to dismiss their power of creation. They perceive themselves as insignificant and powerless, failing to realize that the visible is always a manifestation of the invisible. The real power is nonphysical and is within you; it comes from your mind, not from the external world.

The truth is, your environment is largely a reflection of yourself. It tends to give you what you give yourself first. The more you respect yourself, the more people respect you. When you don't respect yourself, people are more likely to treat you as a doormat. The more you love yourself, the more you allow people to love you. The more you can keep your promise to yourself, the more others trust you.

More generally, as you change your thoughts and expand your vision, your environment will change, too. People will start behaving differently and you will meet new people that support your growth. You may be promoted at work or come across new opportunities. In short, when you become a different person, your environment reflects those changes.

Consider your thoughts as seeds that need to be watered regularly if they are to flourish. Or, if you prefer, think of them as sunrays that become exponentially more powerful with the use of a magnifying glass—your focus. When you focus on a specific thought consistently and for long enough—from a few months to a few years—you will eventually turn it into a tangible thing in this world. This is how every man-made thing was created.

If you've been in the same environment for years, unable to get out of it, ask yourself why this is the case. What needs to change in you for things to improve for you? What do you need to focus on?

I recommend you adopt the following assumption:

As I change, my environment also changes.

Exercise:

What could you do to change yourself (and change your environment)? Come up with a couple of simple things you could do to start changing your life.

Negative assumption #6—I need to be realistic

Have you ever been told to be realistic?

Everybody has a different sense of what is possible in this world. Most people operate on the assumption that most of the things they want are not realistic. Meanwhile, other people are making it happen. Your assumptions determine what you can accomplish. If you listen to everybody around you and adjust your mindset to their (small) thinking, guess what? You won't accomplish much.

If I had listened to people around me, I wouldn't have quit my job to create my own business. Even today, family members and friends tell me some of my goals are impossible. They try to limit me in many ways. They want to reduce my field of possibility, my potential, to match theirs. This often happens unconsciously. The truth is you're already underestimating what you're capable of achieving. Why limit yourself even more by allowing other people to define what you can and cannot do?

I believe your number one priority should be to surround yourself with people who lift you up and encourage you to be the best person you can possibly be. You want to be with people who see more in yourself than you do. When people demand more, you'll raise your standards to match their expectations. The two most important things you must upgrade to change your life are your own psychology—your belief system, emotional well-being, attitude etc.—and your environment. The good news is that your psychology will change almost automatically as you find yourself with the right people in the right environment.

Remember, whatever you think you can do now, you are capable of achieving more. Whatever fear you have, you can overcome it. Whatever limiting belief binds you, you can break through. And whatever you need to know, you can learn. There is no need to be "realistic" here. Be as unrealistic as you want to be!

I recommend you adopt the following assumption:

I create my own reality. What other people believe I can or cannot do is irrelevant.

Exercise:

Answer the following question: in what way are you holding back your potential due to the limitations imposed on you by others?

Negative assumption #7—If I received more, I would give more

Have you ever thought you would work harder if you were paid more? Have you ever said you would invest more in yourself if you had more money?

Now, what if you're never paid more? Are you going to do the bare minimum for the rest of your life? You can, but you'll likely be paid the same ten years from now.

Are you going to wait until you get a pay rise to hire a coach, purchase an improvement program or educate yourself in ways needed to achieve your future goals?

The idea that you'll give more of something once you receive more of it is limiting. It ties in to the belief that one day you'll be ready. One day you'll finally have enough money to invest in yourself.

One day you'll finally get paid enough to give your very best. This way of thinking is backward.

Now, what if you held the assumption that by giving more, you'll receive more. By investing more in yourself, you'll receive more joy, money, confidence or all three. By doing your best at work, you'll be promoted, move on to a better job or create your own business. By helping people and giving more, you'll end up receiving more in the long term.

I encourage you to start giving more and see what happens. Consider adopting the following assumption:

By giving more, I open myself to receiving more.

Exercise:

Answer the following question: What is one thing you could give more of?

Negative assumption #8—Having (too many) problems is a problem

People often assume that problems shouldn't exist and believe they will be happy once they overcome all their challenges. However, in reality, problems are life itself. It doesn't matter how smart, handsome, wealthy and famous you become, you will still go through tough times. For instance, you may have health, relationships or money issues, or you may be shy and insecure.

Trying to escape your problems and believing that one day, once you remove all of them, you'll finally be happy is a poor strategy. Even if you could, other complications would appear.

Now, it is important to realize that problems are subjective. They arise from expectations and false assumptions, not from the way reality is. That's why you can put two people in the same situation, one will be fine, the other will seem to experience a lot of troubles.

For instance:

- If you believe you need to be married before the age of thirty and you aren't, you might perceive that as a problem.
- If you believe you need to make a certain amount of money to feel secure, when you make less, you'll constantly worry about it.
- If you believe you need to be more handsome and aren't, you'll see that as an issue.
- If you believe you should be a certain body weight and aren't, you'll probably feel bad about yourself and have self-esteem issues.

In short, many problems exist only in the human mind, and they depend on the way we interpret what happens to us. For instance, rain can be seen as a problem if you plan to go on a picnic, but it can be seen as a blessing if you are a farmer during a drought.

A great question to ask yourself when you face a problem is, "What do I need to believe to perceive this particular situation as a problem?" As you do this, you'll start realizing that your interpretation of the event causes the suffering, not the event itself. Change the way you interpret the event, and the issue will disappear—or at the very least, it will become more manageable.

As such, having too many problems is not an issue in itself. It's usually a sign that you need to look deeper at the assumptions behind each of your problems. You're probably trying too hard to fight reality. And, there is no doubt, reality wins every time.

Here is a new assumption you can adopt:

Having problems is normal. The less attached I am to my problems, the more irrelevant they become.

Another way to reframe problems or challenges is to perceive them as opportunities. I believe that within every problem lies an opportunity. A problem might offer you an opportunity to make changes in your life. For instance, it might help you learn something about yourself, allowing you to become more peaceful and happier. Or it might make you wiser. Even if you can't see any opportunity, consider these two assumptions:

With any problem comes a new opportunity

Problems are problems and must be avoided

Which one of those assumption is the more empowering? Which one will help you design your ideal life and allow you to live at peace with yourself? Again, the role of your assumptions is to empower you. Whether they are actually true or not is mostly irrelevant.

In fact, seemingly false assumptions, when believed enough, often become self-fulfilling prophecies. Think of visionaries. By setting a clear vision and committing to making it happen, these individuals create a new reality that wasn't there initially. They didn't wait to see it to believe it, they believed it and therefore ended up seeing it. For instance, Elon Musk, whose mission is to colonize Mars, believed he could create a reusable space shuttle that would take off and land. Despite all the critics and multiple setback along the way, he eventually reached this goal.

You can adopt the following assumption:

In any problem lies an opportunity.

Exercise:

Make a list of all your problems. How could you reframe them so they become less of a problem, or even have them open doors to new opportunities?

Negative assumption #9—Things "should" be a certain way

Most people hold the assumption that things should be a certain way. This happens each time you use the world "should."

- There should be no war.
- There should be no famine.
- Corruption shouldn't exist.
- People should be nice to me.
- People should keep their promises.
- I shouldn't have to do X, Y, Z.
- My friends should encourage me instead of putting me down.
- My colleagues should cooperate with me.

These things seem to make sense and would be ideal. Unfortunately, reality is what is, not what you think it should be.

People's desire to argue with reality is understandable but creates more challenges than it fixes. There is no need to argue with reality, nor is there any benefit. Whenever you argue with reality, you lose. Whenever you refuse to see things as they are but as you want them to be, you suffer. As long as you try to deny reality, you'll struggle. Reality just *is* and can't be any other way. It's never wrong, and it's never a problem.

Consider the following examples:

I work so hard. I should be making twice as much money.

Reality: you don't.

What does believing you should make twice as much money do to your happiness and peace of mind? How does it serve you?

There should be no war.

Reality: wars are happening right now.

What does believing there should be no war do to your happiness and peace of mind? Does it even encourage you do something about it?

People should keep their promises.

Reality: most people don't.

What does such a belief do for your happiness and peace of mind? Does it help you?

Believing things should be different is as ridiculous as believing a $1 bill should be a $100 bill. A $1 bill *is* a $1 bill, and it is that way, whether you like it or not. Why? Simply because it is!

Accepting things as they are doesn't mean you need to like them. I don't like wars, but they're happening regardless. I don't want people to die from starvation, but people still do. Reality doesn't give a damn about my opinion on how things should be. It doesn't report to me.

The bottom line is this: whatever is happening is supposed to be happening. Every bit of it. Why? Because it's happening. If it shouldn't, it wouldn't.

I understand this concept may be difficult to grasp but can you see how important it is? It means you can start releasing and redirecting all the energy you're currently using trying to change the present reality.

Now, does that mean you have no power to change the world

whatsoever? Absolutely not. While you have no power to change what is, you can change what *will be* through your actions.

There is a big misconception that if you accept reality as it is, you're not doing anything about it. This is false. Ironically, the opposite is true: the more you accept reality as it is, the more power you have to change it. Conversely, the more you assume things should be a certain way, the less power you have.

Thus, *the first step to changing anything in your life is to accept it as part of your reality right now*. Accept it exactly as it is. For instance, rather than thinking you should lose twenty pounds, accept that you weigh exactly what you're supposed to weigh right now. Why? Because that's what the scale indicates! Once you've accepted that reality, you can reformulate your statement as follows: I *could* lose twenty pounds. And from that place, you can start taking action to create a new reality. Again, it might seem contradictory, but you don't change reality by believing things should be different. Instead, you change reality by accepting it exactly as it is, while envisioning how things could be in the future.

Could vs. should

As we've seen, an effective way to change our thinking is by replacing the world "should" with the word "could". Below are some examples:

There *should* be no war (denial of reality). —> There *could* be no war (openness to a future possibilities).

I work so hard, I *should* be making twice as much money (denial of reality). —> I work so hard, I *could* be making twice as much money (openness to future possibilities). You could probably make twice as much money but for that, you have to design a plan to achieve that goal.

People *should* keep their promises (denial of reality). —> People *could* keep their promises (openness to future possibilities). Yes, they could. Will they? Perhaps. Maybe they would if you asked them in a different way. Or they may become reliable one day and start keeping their promises. Who knows?

My friends *should* encourage me instead of putting me down (denial of reality). —> My friends *could* encourage me instead of putting me down (openness to future possibilities). Maybe you could make it clear that you want them to support you. You could even tell them exactly how you would like them to give you their support. They may end up encouraging you—or not.

As you can see, "should" is not an empowering word. I hope by now you realize that wanting reality to be different doesn't empower you to change it. If anything, it makes you resentful, powerless or angry, and it can disturb your peace of mind. Wouldn't you feel more at peace if you accepted reality is exactly as it should be?

On the other hand, "could" creates options and possibilities. It opens you up to new actions and encourages you to make changes. When you use the word "could", you assume things are as they are now, but they may change in the future.

- Yes, people could do X, Y, Z under different circumstances —but they don't right now.
- Yes, there could be no war or famine in the future—but people are fighting wars right now.
- Yes, your friends could encourage you—but they don't right now.

I would like you to start taking notice whenever you use the word "should." Perhaps you tell yourself the story that you should work harder or that you should be smarter or better in some way.

Realize this is a false assumption. You are exactly as you're supposed to be now and there is nothing wrong with that. Yes, you could work harder, become smarter or improve yourself in countless ways, and if you're determined to do so, you will.

The new assumption you can adopt is:

I fully accept what is, and I can create what will be.

Exercise:

Make a list of five things you believe should be a certainty but aren't right now. Then, replace "should" with "could". How does it make you feel?

Negative assumption #10—My past equals my future

Do you live in the past? That is, do you still carry with you the same assumptions that created your past?

Your past in no way predicts your future. It only seems that way because you keep operating with the same system (i.e., you keep holding the same assumptions). As the saying goes, if you keep doing what you've always done, you'll keep getting the same results. To change your life, you must change your assumptions, which means changing your beliefs, and changing your actions.

Let's say you're currently overweight. If I were to implant the belief system of a personal trainer in your brain, what do you think would happen? You would lose your weight quickly. It would be inevitable. If you're struggling financially and were to wake up tomorrow with the exact same mindset as a multi-millionaire, you would quickly start earning more money. This would also be inevitable. This is because, with a different set of beliefs, you cannot help but take different actions and thus obtain different results.

In the end, what you do every day—starting from today—will determine your future. Armed with your new empowering assumptions, you have the power to think, feel and act differently. As you do so, you'll be able to alter the course of your life and obtain better outcome as a result. You're largely the product of what you think every day. As the Buddha supposedly said, *what you think, you become.*" Replace old assumptions with more empowering ones, and your future will change.

Another way to look at your past is to think of it as a "sunk cost"— a cost that can't be recovered. This is a common term used in business. What if you could see your past as a sunk cost? How much lighter would you feel? This approach is what the success expert Brian Tracy calls "zero-based thinking."

To apply zero-based thinking in your life ask yourself:

"Knowing what I know now, what are some of the things I'm currently doing that I wouldn't continue?"

Below are some more specific questions:

- Knowing what I know now, would I still launch that new product? If your answer is no, you'd need to discontinue the product launch.
- Knowing what I know now, would I be in this relationship? If your answer is no, you'd need to muster up the courage to end it.
- Knowing what I know now, would I take my current job? If your answer is no, you'd need to find a new job.
- Knowing what I know now, should I stay the same? If the answer is no, you'd need to start making changes in your life.

What about you? Knowing what you know now, what are you going to start doing differently today? Knowing your current disempowering assumptions, what new assumptions will you adopt?

The bottom line is you can make changes at any time. The belief that your past determines your future is just that, a belief—and an erroneous one. Your past by no mean equals your future. You have the power to reframe your life and start anew from today. What you start doing from today will create your future. So, forget past mistakes. Instead, start thinking as the person you want to become and act that way—from today.

Your new assumption:

Every day I start anew, free of all past burdens.

Exercise:

Close your eyes and imagine you could start your day free of any burden from the past. How would it make you feel?

Something is wrong with me/I'm not good enough

Negative assumption #11—I'm not good enough

Do you feel unworthy? Do you believe something is wrong with you and nothing you can do will ever fix it?

For some reason, many people believe something is inherently wrong with them. They feel as though they are a fraud. No matter what they do or how hard they try, they always fall short. As a result, they keep seeking external validation, hoping something outside of them will finally make them "good enough."

What if this is nothing more than an erroneous assumption? When you were born, did the doctor tell your parents, "I'm sorry but your son/daughter won't be good enough."?

What does not being good enough even mean? This is probably the first question you want to answer. In the end, it's all a matter of perspective and boils down to the way you choose to interpret what happens to you. Edison "failed" thousands of times when trying to invent the light bulb. Imagine if each time he "failed" he told himself how stupid he was? Do you think he would have been able to persevere?

The truth is most successful people have failed hundreds, if not thousands of times in their lives. However, they perceive failure in a different way than most people. For them, they just tried something, and it didn't work out as planned. Unsuccessful people might add, "therefore I failed" or even worse, "therefore I'm a failure" to the statement and build a whole story around it.

Failure is never personal. Whether you fail one time, or thousands of times has nothing to do with who you are as a person. At the core, you're still the same individual. No amount of failure can ever make you a failure. The only reason you feel like a failure is because you hold false assumptions. The only real failure is not learning from your mistakes. As long as you constantly seek to learn and improve, failure does not exist. Period.

The bottom line is you don't need to do something to be good enough, and "failures" can't make you a lesser person. The only thing you need to do is to change your perspective and adopt different assumptions. Below are some empowering assumptions to adopt:

I'm good enough for now.

This presupposes that, 1) I'm good enough and, 2) I can always improve whenever is needed.

I like this one. I used to have unrealistic expectations and beat myself up each time I wasn't living up to them. Now, I just assume everything I do is good enough *for now*. I don't think my work should be better. In fact, it is exactly as it should be now. Why? Because it is how it is. Sure, it might not be as good as I would like it to be in the ideal world but, over time, I can always improve.

I'm perfect in my imperfections.

No matter what you think, you're not broken, and you don't need to be fixed. The same way failure is not something separated from success, your imperfections aren't preventing you from being perfect and whole. They are part of your perfection.

My intent is pure.

Whatever the external results, we usually have good intentions, and this alone is a wonderful reason to celebrate ourselves. I believe the size of your bank account or your status is irrelevant. Your intention is what matters most. During challenging times, I remind myself that my intentions are pure, and I acknowledge myself for that. What about you? Could you take a few seconds now to give yourself a pat on the back and acknowledge your intention to better yourself and do good in the world?

I matter.

In case nobody told you that before, you matter! With that and the pat you just give yourself on the back, you must feel wonderful now! It's okay to be proud of yourself and celebrate your life. As time passes, I've learned to celebrate my accomplishments—both small and big—because, if I don't celebrate myself and my life, in most cases, nobody else will.

In fact, for people to value you and respect you, it is important you value yourself first. If you don't set boundaries and standards in your life, people will end up disrespecting you. You matter, so celebrate every one of your accomplishments and give yourself motivational rewards each time you achieve your goals. The more you focus on your accomplishments and all the things you're doing well, the better you'll feel about yourself. And the better you feel about yourself, the more likely you are to feel good about others, too.

You also need to understand it is possible to be a high achiever and still feel as though something is wrong with you. That is very common. It shows that self-worth is not linked to what you do—although it does play a role—but to what you choose to focus on, acknowledge and celebrate.

People with a healthy self-esteem constantly focus on the things they're doing well. They celebrate their successes and shrug it off when things don't go as planned. In other words, they have a biased (but positive) way to look at their life and a selective memory. They give little importance to negative things and focus their attention on all the positive aspects of their lives.

Conversely, people who don't feel good enough, focus on all the things they're doing wrong and dwell on negative events. Even when good things happen, they dismiss them as being no big deal and, instead, focus only on the things they could have done better —because, from their perspective, they aren't good enough.

For more on how to overcome feelings of unworthiness, refer to my book, *Master Your Emotions: A Practical Guide to Overcome Negativity and Better Manage Your Feelings.*

Exercise:

Look at one area in which you tend to blame yourself for not being good enough. Now, say to yourself, "I'm good enough for now." Then, take a step back and put things in perspective. Realize how much room you have to improve and how much time you have to do so. You're good enough *for now*. You can always improve yourself in the future if needed.

Negative assumption #12—I will believe it when I see it

Many people fail to realize how much power they have to create their future. They don't understand that, by believing enough in something, they can create it. If they were to decide today how they want their future to look in five or ten years—and resolve to make it a reality—they would likely end up where they intended to be.

What if instead of thinking you'll believe it when you see it, you decide you'll see it when you believe it?

What do you want to believe hard enough to be able to see in the future?

Consider adopting the following assumption:

I believe it therefore I'll see it.

Exercise:

Think of one thing you really want to make happen in the future. Hold the space for it. Make it part of your field of possibilities. Ask yourself:

What if I could create it?

What if it is possible?

Negative assumption #13—I'm not ready yet

Have you ever postponed something because you didn't feel ready? Perhaps you believed you needed more training or the timing wasn't right.

In my experience, there is no such thing as being one hundred percent ready for anything. There will never be a "right time" to quit your job, start a business or enter a new relationship. You can always find excuses to put off things you're scared to do, and that's what most people end up doing. However, in reality, the best time is often now. As the proverb says, the best time to plant a tree was twenty years ago, the second-best time is now.

Muscles only grow when they are under pressure, and the same is true of human beings. When we move beyond our comfort zones and do something a little scary, we start growing. This doesn't happen when we're perfectly ready. When we start stepping out of our comfort zones we can grow more in one year than we normally would in ten years. In fact, there is no other way. Working hard on ourselves and facing our fears little by little is the only way we can discover our true capabilities. Remember the best time is now!

Look at some of your goals or dreams and ask yourself, "What if I could start now?" Here is the thing: you can always start right away. There is always one simple step you can take to start moving toward your goals.

Adopt the following assumption:

Because I start before I'm ready, I can achieve anything I want faster than I ever thought possible.

Exercise:

Identify one thing you haven't done (yet) because it makes you feel a little uncomfortable. Hold the space for it to happen in the near future.

Could you do it?

Will you?

Negative assumption #14—If I believe it, I can achieve it

This assumption ties in to the previous one. When you feel unprepared, you assume you don't believe enough in yourself or in your goals to achieve the results you're after. Therefore, you must do more visualization, recite more affirmations, gain more experience or get more training. In short, you must be confident of success before you can achieve your goal. Or so you think.

But what if this is pure BS? What if you don't need to believe in something to achieve it? In fact, that may be one of the biggest lies you've been told in your life. This lie could prevent you achieving everything you want in life.

This type of thinking is a cognitive distortion called "emotional reasoning", which means believing your emotions are telling the truth. In this case, because of fear and self-doubt, you assume you're not ready to raise your price, ask for a raise, ask someone out or ask for whatever else you want to receive.

Fortunately, you are *not* your emotions or your beliefs. You don't need to believe something to actually achieve it. For instance, you can ask for a raise and get it regardless of your level of confidence. Sure, the more confident you are, the better, but there is no rule that says you need to believe in something before you can receive it. As the founder of Virgin Group, Richard Branson, said, "*If somebody offers you an amazing opportunity but you are not sure you can do it, say yes—then learn how to do it later!*"

The bottom line is you can ask for things you want even if you don't believe you can receive them. You'll be surprised by what you can receive and achieve by doing so. Remember, it's normal to feel nervous when you try something new. This doesn't mean you should study more or wait until you have an unshakable belief in yourself before doing it. If anything, by doing it, you'll gain confidence in yourself. Confidence is built through action.

Here is a new assumption I encourage you to adopt:

I go after what I want, regardless of how confident I feel.

Here's a bonus assumption:

Action cures fear.

Exercise:

Think of one thing you believe is impossible. It could be something you want to ask for or something you want to do. Could you challenge yourself to do it? Will you?

Negative assumption #15—It's just who I am

"I'm shy, it is just who I am."

"I'm stupid, it is just who I am."

How often have you used such statements in the past? Have you noticed that you rarely use either expression to express positive sides of your personality? You seldom say:

- "I'm awesome, it is just who am."
- "I'm smart, it is just who I am."
- "I'm kind and generous, it is just who I am."

"It's just who I am" is more than an assumption you hold. It's a convenient excuse you use to avoid making changes. It's another way you narrow down your field of possibilities. If you believe shyness is part of your identity, how likely are you to overcome it? If you perceive yourself as being stupid, what are the chances you'll keep persevering and learn from your mistakes?

Your self-perception influences your decisions and ultimately creates your own reality but, often, this self-perception is nothing more than a story you use to avoid making painful changes in your life.

I'd like to suggest a better assumption:

I'm the scriptwriter of my life and can rewrite any story I wish.

Exercise:

What disempowering story have you been telling yourself for years? What if the opposite is true? Come up with twenty reasons why this story may not be true.

Negative assumption #16—I lack motivation/I'm lazy

People often struggle with motivation. They see themselves as lazy and beat themselves up as a result. But is it true? Are they lazy? I don't believe in laziness. While it is true some people are less motivated than others, people who struggle with motivation usually lack a *motive for action*. They lack a larger purpose behind what they do. If you look at people who are passionate, they seldom lack motivation. They are naturally motivated and pulled toward their vision. This is because they have a *motive for action*.

If you lack motivation it may be because you're doing the wrong things or you're doing them for the wrong reasons (e.g., reasons that don't inspire you). Therefore, the first step to motivate yourself is to find out the "why" behind your goal. Why are you pursuing a particular goal? What values do you attach to it and what benefit will you receive from achieving it?

For instance:

If you want to lose weight, why does that matter? Why is that new identity of "being a fit, slim and healthy person" important to you?

If you lack motivation at your current job, ask yourself why is this job important? What is your bigger vision behind it? If you don't enjoy your job, what could you do to feel more motivated?

- Could you change the way you do things?
- Could you work on different projects?
- Could you see your current job as a stepping stone toward your dream career? If so, how?

The second step is to start taking small actions consistently every day. The more progress you make, the more confident and disciplined you become.

Here is a new assumption you can adopt:

I'm motivated because I have a motive for action.

To learn how to find what you love and make a living out of it, refer to my book, *The Passion Manifesto: Escape the Rat Race, Uncover Your Passion and Design a Career and Life You Love.*

Exercise:

Look at one area of your life in which you lack motivation. Now, try to identify why that's the case. Is it because you have no interest? Is it because it isn't aligned with your deepest values?

Negative assumption #17—Self-discipline sucks

Do you hate self-discipline? Do you want to live your life on your own terms without having to follow a rigid schedule?

Have you ever examined what a lack of self-discipline costs you? Do you realize that with enough self-discipline you could achieve almost anything you want in life?

Often, people crave more freedom and perceive self-discipline as something that robs them of their freedom. But is that so? How much freedom do you have if you can't discipline yourself to do what you need do to create the life you want? Is being overweight because you lack the self-discipline to eat healthily a sign of great personal freedom? Is procrastinating on important tasks what you would call freedom? And I'm not even talking about the emotional cost of a lack of self-discipline, which often includes low self-esteem, lack of motivation and the absence of a clear purpose in life.

If you have little control over your body, your mind and your emotional state, can you really be free? I believe freedom is the ability to have absolute control over our mind, body and emotional state, and this all starts with self-discipline.

As the motivational speaker Les Brown said, "*Do what is easy and your life will be hard. Do what is hard and your life becomes easy.*"

When you can discipline yourself to do what is necessary when you need to do it—whether you feel like it or not—you'll experience freedom and will achieve incredible things. As a result, your life will become easier.

You can adopt the following assumptions:

Self-discipline equals freedom. With enough self-discipline, I can achieve anything I want.

For more on how to develop self-discipline, refer to my book, *Upgrade Yourself: Simple Strategies to Transform Your Mindset, Improve Your Habits, and Change Your Life.*

Exercise:

Imagine if you could do all the things you know you should be doing. How would you feel? What difference would it make to your life? What single habit could help you build self-discipline?

To help you implement a powerful morning ritual you'll keep for many years, feel free to refer to my book, *Wake Up Call: How to Take Control of Your Morning and Transform Your Life.*

Negative assumption #18—It's selfish to focus on myself

Do you believe focusing on yourself is selfish? What if the opposite is actually true?

If you've taken an airplane before, you've probably listened to the procedure to follow in case of an emergency. Do you remember what you're supposed to do to ensure the safety of your children in a case of an emergency? You're supposed to take care of yourself first by putting on your oxygen mask. Then, and only then, can you take care of your children and ensure their safety. The same can be said for life in general.

If you don't focus on yourself, learn more about yourself and cater to your own needs, how can you support other people and bring out the best in them? Jim Rohn, the motivational speaker said, *"I'll take care of me for you, if you will please take care of you for me."* What a wonderful statement. How can you take care of other people if you don't take care of yourself first?

- Do you make other people suffer because of your inability to deal with negative emotions?
- Does your lack of self-understanding prevent you from being your best?
- Does your poor health and lack of energy negatively impact your family?

Imagine how much better off your family and friends would be if you were happy, healthy, energetic and living your life on purpose? In fact, one of the best gifts you can give people you love is your personal development.

As you focus on becoming a better person, everybody around you will benefit. Thus, focusing on yourself is not selfish. If anything, it is selfless. What if you replace the assumption, *I'll take care of you* with, *I'll take care of me for you*? What difference would this make to your life and to your family, friends or colleagues' lives?

You can adopt the following assumption:

I take care of me for *my family and friends.*

Exercise:

Identify one quality that, if you were to develop it, would have a positive impact on people around you. It could be keeping better control over your anger, keeping your promises, becoming a better listener, stopping criticizing people, etc.

Negative assumption #19—I'm too old

I wish I received a $100 bill each time someone told me they're too old to learn a foreign language, travel, change their career or learn whatever it is they want to learn. I hate when people tell me they're too old to do something. Why? Because it is usually not true.

The assumption "I'm too old" is a defense mechanism people use to avoid facing the truth. In fact, what most people really mean when they say, "I'm too old," is one or several of the following things:

- I don't believe in myself (anymore).
- I'd rather buy into the story I'm too old than to admit I just gave up on myself.
- I'm not willing to put a lot of effort into something that may not work out.
- I'm actually not that interested in doing the thing I say I

want to do. I just pretend I am to strengthen my victim mentality and keep feeling sorry for myself.

In short, "I'm too old" is another story you're telling yourself. I understand you may be too old to become an NBA player or an Olympic athlete, but you're not too old to achieve most of your goals and dreams. The issue here is a lack of commitment. Do you really want it? If so, what price are you willing to pay?

If you don't want to pay the price, that's fine—but don't moan about it. Your time and resources are limited, and you must use them wisely. Just be honest with yourself.

You can adopt the following assumption:

I'm never too old to do what I want to do.

Exercise:

Have you ever told yourself you're too old to pursue your goals? If so, identify one goal you talked yourself out of because you considered yourself too old. Go to your favorite search engine and search for "old" people who have accomplished that same goal. For instance, search "oldest people" + your goal.

Negative assumption #20—Telling the truth hurts people and should be avoided

Are you afraid to tell the truth because it could hurt or upset people? Now, is the fear of hurting people the real problem here? Often, it isn't. In fact, not telling the truth is often what ends up hurting people the most.

The main reasons we don't tell the truth is not to avoid hurting people, but:

- to avoid facing rejection, and

- because it's uncomfortable for us.

In short, lying or omitting the truth is an easy way out. Now, you might think, "okay, I admit, I don't always tell the truth, but it's not a big deal, right?" Wrong. Very wrong.

I would argue that not telling the truth is an act of selfishness disguised as an act of courtesy. When you refuse to tell the truth and fail to give people honest feedback, you rob them of a valuable opportunity to grow and correct erroneous behaviors they may not even be aware of. You don't provide them with the external perspective they need to improve.

But that's not all. Not being honest with people also prevents you from building more meaningful relationships. Sadly, most of our relationships are superficial. The typical relationship goes as follows: I rub your back, you rub my back, and everybody is happy. That's great because nobody needs to:

- Be vulnerable
- Uncover deeply rooted fears and work on overcoming them
- Take the risk of offending the other person, or
- Be disapproved of or even rejected.

Telling the truth is necessary to grow and overcome your problems. Most people pretend everything is okay when they know deep down it isn't. By failing to tell the truth, they build resentment and are unable to have healthy relationships. In romantic relationships, we're often scared to say what we really think. By shutting ourselves off and failing to share how we feel, we build resentment which, over time, can negatively impact the relationship and may even destroy it. Doing this, we selfishly rob the other person—who is often unaware of the situation—of the opportunity to change his or her behavior. We may also interpret things incorrectly, not even realizing our partner has good intentions. It might just be a misunderstanding. Unless we share our feelings and concerns, we can't clear the misunderstanding, which may fester over time.

To me, there is nothing more annoying than not being told the truth. I want to improve whenever I can. If I'm not told the truth, if I'm unaware of my shortcomings, changing them is difficult, if not impossible. Even if the truth can be painful, it always serves well me long term. Think about it. If you've been doing something wrong, would you prefer someone telling you right away or learning it years later?

The bottom line is, omitting the truth is often not about protecting other people's feelings; it's about avoiding making ourselves vulnerable and/or avoiding being rejected. We don't omit the truth in the interest of the other person, but in our own selfish interest.

When we tell the truth, we put other's interests before ours, which requires tremendous courage and concern for the other person. Yes, telling the truth and hearing it can be scary, but it can also be extremely powerful. Telling the truth creates meaningful relationships, develops trust and gives others the opportunity to grow and improve so they can reach their full potential.

Also, the beauty of truth is that it destroys everything we are not, such as our delusions and limiting beliefs—sometimes via a painful process—and reveals to us what we really are.

You can adopt the following assumption:

I help others and myself grow by telling the truth whenever possible.

Exercise:

Answer the following question: If you could tell only one truth you haven't told before, who would be the person you would tell it to and what would that be?

48

5

ASSUMPTIONS ABOUT SUCCESS

Do you want to be successful? Do you want to design a life you don't need to escape from? Unfortunately, you may have many assumptions that prevent you from attaining the level of success you want. In this section, we'll look at some of the most disempowering assumptions about success and see how you can shift your perspective and adopt more empowering ones.

Let's get started.

Negative assumption #21—Success is possible

Do you believe that success is possible? If so, you're more likely to succeed than people who believe success is out of reach. However, what if this assumption is actually limiting you? Is it possible to replace it with a more empowering one?

After reading over a hundred books on personal development, I came to the initial conclusion that success is highly predictable and luck only plays a small part. While we may fail repeatedly in the short term, as long as we keep moving toward our goals, learning from our mistakes and making the necessary adjustments along the journey, we're "very likely" to achieve our long-term goals. "Success is very likely" is how I felt until I came across Christian Mickelsen, a coach who says the following:

 I really believe that results are inevitable if people are willing to do the work. If you keep taking action and you keep working on your inner game stuff and you never give up, you will achieve your results. It's just a matter of time.

Immediately, I thought, "*What a great assumption!*"

What if you replace the assumption, "success is very likely" with, "success is inevitable?" How do you think it would impact your level of confidence and the actions you take? What if by working hard on your goal—and most importantly working hard on yourself—success was just a matter of time? After all, you can always learn from your failures and improve as a result. You can always adapt your strategy and make adjustments as you proceed. And what prevents you from receiving help from people who have already achieved your goals?

As Tony Robbins says, "*Resourcefulness is the ultimate resource,*" and with enough passion, motivation, determination, love, creativity and desire to contribute, you can attract all the resources you need to help you achieve your goal. You have another great assumption here.

Perhaps you feel this is far-fetched. Now, the question is, would adopting such an assumption increase the chances of achieving your goals? If so, would you rather believe that success is possible or inevitable?

Here is the assumption you can adopt:

With perseverance, success is inevitable.

Exercise:

Look at your biggest goal or dream. Now, imagine you were absolutely convinced success was inevitable. How would this make you feel? What action(s) would you take? Spend a couple of minutes playing that scenario in your mind.

Negative assumption #22—Success is having more

A widely spread definition of success is having more material things, such as a bigger house, a better car, more expensive clothes. While all these things are nice, it's a very limited view of success.

Success is not about what you have, it's about who you become.

Striving to become more by removing your fears and limitations so you can express the essence of who you are in all its magnificence is a better definition of success, isn't it?

What if you could become fearless, remove self-doubt and procrastination and help more people than you could ever imagine? What if you could feel great about yourself every day? What would this mindset do for you? Perhaps success is not even about becoming anything, but more about removing what you are *not*, to let who you *are* shine through.

This is why having stretching goals that inspire you is so invaluable. To achieve difficult goals, you need to become a better person.

You can adopt the following assumption:

Success is not about what I have, it's about who I become.

Exercise:

Look at the bigger vision you have for yourself. Now, write down all the qualities and skills the future you would embody.

Negative assumption #23—Success is an outcome

If you believe that success is an outcome, you'll constantly chase it and will never catch it. You'll be seeking more but failing to appreciate all the things you already have.

Success is not an outcome. There is no end to it. Success is who you are every day. It's a way of being. It is a constant work in progress. If you do your best every day and implement solid habits that move you closer to your ideal life, you're already successful. As the motivational speaker, Earl Nightingale, said, "*Success is the progressive realization of a worthy goal or ideal.*" Please note, he didn't say success is the achievement of your goal, but he said it is the progressive realization of the goal.

I suggest you adopt the following assumption:

I'm moving toward my goal, therefore I'm successful.

Exercise:

Based on your current goals, write down your ideal successful day —what you would need to do to feel like a success every day. Select a few simple habits that move you toward this goal. Start with tiny daily goals and achieve them for thirty days. This will help you build more confidence and increase your self-esteem.

Negative assumption #24—Failure is the opposite of success

What if you fail? Most people are afraid of trying something new in case they fail. They identify with their past failure and declare, "*I am a failure.*" But what really happens when you fail? *You tried something, and it didn't work out as expected*. That's it. Is that such a terrible thing?

You've probably been taught there is success on one side and failure on the other. This couldn't be further from the truth. In reality, success and failure work hand in hand. Success is a process and this process includes so-called failures. You don't succeed by avoiding failure, you actually "fail your way to success." This is the only way to succeed. Therefore, failure is nothing more than *a built-in feedback mechanism that is part of the process leading to success.* Failing is merely receiving feedback that what you're trying to do doesn't work and you need to change something. That's all there is to it. Anything else is a story in your mind. If you can change the way you perceive failure, you can achieve almost anything you want.

Unsurprisingly, successful people have a different relationship with failure. They don't seek to avoid mistakes. On the contrary, they expect to fail many times before reaching their goals. If anything, they try to fail more and earlier, when making mistakes isn't as costly. As a result, by the time they achieve their goals, they have probably "failed" hundreds of times more than the average person. Their secret? They don't label their setbacks as "failures" but as stepping stones towards their goals.

I kept falling short of my goals again and again for several years, but I've avoided focusing my attention on those so-called "failures." Instead, I focused on improving my skills while sticking to my vision. I did what I had to do every day to get where I wanted to be. During this journey, I (not so) happily failed my way to success.

The bottom line is that failure and success are two sides of the same coin. You can't have one without the other, and neither of them is good or bad.

Whenever you "fail" say to yourself:

- I just tried something, and it didn't work out as planned. Next!
- I just tried something, and it didn't work out as planned. Let me learn from it and try again.

Here is a new assumption for you:

I happily fail my way to success. I fail faster and better each time.

Exercise:

Clear your mind and connect with your deepest sense of self. Now, realize that none of the "failures" from your past have ever done anything to you. And no failure will ever. This is a very powerful realization.

Negative assumption #25—I'm either a success or a failure

Often people adopt a black and white vision of things. They set a goal and when they don't reach it, they declare themselves a failure. Perhaps they wanted to lose twenty pounds but only lose five. Or they only make one quarter of the amount of money they wanted to generate with their side business. In reality, anyone who makes progress can't be a failure. A better reaction would be to celebrate their success and look back at how far they've already gone. The truth is you can't always achieve every goal as fast as you would like to. That's why it is so important to focus on the process—what you do every day—and be less attached to the outcome, especially if you don't have one hundred percent control over it.

Adopt the following assumption:

I'm successful because I'm making progress toward my goal.

Exercise:

Select one goal you have failed to achieve. It can be a current goal or a past goal. Focus on what you did well. What progress did you make? What did you learn? What could you acknowledge about yourself? Was your intent pure?

Negative assumption #26 - I need to be lucky to be successful

Do you play the lottery hoping to become rich one day? That's extremely unlikely. Not because the odds are against you (they are) but because you believe in luck to begin with.

In fact, I believe self-made millionaires (before becoming wealthy) are significantly less likely to play the lottery than the overall population. Why? Because to get where they are, they had to ignore luck. Ironically, people who choose to play the lottery, because they tend to see success as an "event," have almost no chance of ever becoming rich (except by the exceedingly rare possibility of winning the lottery).

Success is not an "event," it's a process. You don't become wealthy, create an amazing relationship or lose weight by purchasing a $49.99 program online. Otherwise, everybody would have everything they ever wanted. Anything of value takes time and effort. It is the result of a specific process that must be followed diligently over an extensive period of time. (I know. Nothing very sexy here).

Unfortunately, most people have adopted what I call a "lottery mentality." They constantly look for the magic pill that will allow them to achieve results instantly and effortlessly. Let me tell you a secret: *There is no such pill!*

In reality, you don't get what you want by believing in luck and hoping for the best. You must provoke luck by carefully planning what you want and keep pushing until you "get lucky."

To sum up, luck is not an effective strategy on which you can design your life. Don't rely on it. Instead, focus on the process—what you do every day. The process is what allows you to grow and become the person you need to become in order to achieve your goals. Remember, success is not what you have, it is who you become. It's not an event, it's a process.

Here is an empowering assumption to adopt:

I choose to create my own success, regardless of external circumstances.

To learn in more detail how to achieve your most challenging goals, refer to my book, *The One Goal: Master the Art of Goal Setting, Win Your Inner Battles, and Achieve Exceptional Results.*

Exercise:

Imagine there is no such thing as luck and you are guaranteed to achieve anything you want. What would you do?

Negative assumption #27—I'm not there yet

Have you ever felt frustrated knowing you could do so much more? Does this mean you're not there yet? Do you have to beat yourself up every day for not being good enough? What if you change the assumption, *"I'm not there yet"* to, *"I'm already there."*? Is it possible you've already reached your destination and everything else you'll accomplish is icing on the cake?

You can choose to see success as a journey to be enjoyed. Thus, by taking the first step toward your most important goals, you're already successful. People often say they "made it," but nobody really does. You can't make it and just relax for the rest of your life.

Because life is always changing, the only way to feel happy and successful is to keep moving. For instance:

- You don't stop meditating one day because you realize you've done enough of it.
- You can't stop exercising one day and expect to keep the same body and energy levels forever.
- You can't maintain a healthy body by dumping your healthy diet and eating junk food every day.
- You can't stop making an effort in your relationships just because you're now married to the perfect wife/husband.
- You can't stop innovating and improving your services/products and processes just because your business is successful now.

The point is, success is an ongoing process. It's something you do every day, not something you'll reach in five or ten years. How would you feel if you adopted the assumption that by doing your best today to build a better tomorrow, you're already successful?

To be honest, for many months (if not years), I've been frustrated because I "failed" to obtain the results I wanted with my business. While not making enough money has been part of it, the most frustrating aspect was not being able to reach out to more people. As a result, I felt jealous of other peoples' success, believing I deserved it as well. I was angry at myself for not being good enough. However, over time, I made peace with it—at least to a certain extent. To do so, I started questioning my assumptions about success. I realized that perhaps all I had to do was enjoy the journey. Was it possible that I was already successful by doing my best each day?

Your new assumption:

I'm already there, and I'm more than enough for now.

Exercise:

What if you've already arrived? Imagine there was nowhere else to go, nothing more to do to make you happy and complete. You could just release all the tension for one moment. How would it make you feel?

Negative assumption #28—I need to achieve big things to feel like I'm a success

Do you want to make a huge impact on the world and leave a legacy? What if you fail to achieve even ten percent of this goal? Will you spend your entire life feeling as though you aren't good enough?

Many high achievers spend their lives trying to prove to themselves and to the world they are good enough. They fail to appreciate all the things they've already accomplished, focusing only on what they need to accomplish in the future. What if I told you that you don't need to achieve big things to feel like a success?

Let me ask you one question: Would you sell your eyes for one billion dollars? What about your legs? What does that say about the intrinsic value of a human being's life?

What if you change your assumption. Consider the following more powerful assumption:

If I can change the life of one person, even in a minor way, I'm a huge success

Think about it. If all you did in your entire life was to help just one person make some changes in his or her life, couldn't you see yourself as successful?

As I mentioned previously, I used to be frustrated by not being in a position to help as many people as I wanted to. Then, when some of my readers told me I'd made a difference in their lives, I realized I had already become a big success. What more could I ask for?

Another key assumption I hold is:

Having good intentions makes me a massive success.

Too often, we can be frustrated by our lack of results. But what if the key is not the results we obtain, but the intention behind our actions? Unfortunately, we don't have full control over the results we seek, but we can always choose our intentions. Why not see ourselves as a massive success for having noble intentions? After all, aren't we trying to do the best we can at our own level?

What about you? What makes you a big success? Who did you help? Perhaps you helped a family member when they were in trouble. Or maybe you coached someone and made a difference in his or her life. Or perhaps you're doing your best to educate your children. Take some time to acknowledge your accomplishments and accept the positive impact you're having on other people.

You can adopt the assumptions below:

By changing some people's lives, even in a minor way, I'm a huge success.

I have good intentions, therefore I'm a massive success.

Exercise:

Who did you help? Make a list of the people you helped in your life. Now, allow yourself to feel good for having helped these people. How does this make you feel? Aren't you already successful?

Negative assumption #29—I don't have enough

We live in a society where we never seem to have enough. While we enjoy more luxury than kings and queens did a couple of centuries ago, we behave as though we live in scarcity. This is simply not the case. We just lack perspective.

The United Nations Food and Agriculture Organization estimates that about 795 million people were suffering from chronic undernourishment in 2014-2016. Thats' one in nine! According to a 2005 United Nations report, across the world, 1.6 billion people are inadequately housed an 100 million are completely homeless.

In this regard, your current situation is probably not as bad as you think. What if you substitute your current assumption, "I don't have enough," for the formula, "Food + shelter = happiness + success." How much happier would this make you? The bottom line is you don't need to have more to be happier, you simply need to realize how much you already have.

Your new assumption:

Food + shelter = happiness + success.

Exercise:

Visualize all the things you ate today. Then, visualize some of your favorite dishes. Realize how blessed you are to have access to such a variety of dishes. Now, visualize yourself in the comfort of your bed. If that helps, remember a time when you felt so tired you couldn't wait to go to bed. Remember a rainy day or a cold day when all you wanted was to be warm at home. If you wish, you can do this exercise every day in the morning and/or in the evening.

Negative assumption #30—You can't have it all

We often say either something is too good to be true or that we can't have it all. It has to be either or. But is that true? Again, if you assume you can't have it all, how likely are you to do what it takes to attain it? For instance, perhaps you believe you can't both have a job you love and make good money. Or maybe you think you can't have both a successful career and free time to spend with your family. It has to be one or the other. Now, what if you could have a great job *and* make money; have a successful career *and* a lot of free time?

A great question to ask yourself is, "How can I get both? How can I have this *and* that?" Just by changing your assumption, you'll think differently and take actions that will help you achieve better results.

Your new assumption is therefore:

I can have it all.

Exercise:

Visualize what it would look like if you had it all (whatever that means to you). Keep that vision as a possible future. Hold the space for it in your mind.

Negative assumption #31 - I can't ask for what I want

You likely hold the assumption that you shouldn't ask for what you want. After all, when you were a kid, you wanted all kind of things but were told again and again:

"No, don't do this."

"Don't do that."

"You can't have this."

"Put that down."

As a result, by the time you reached your teenage years, you'd internalized the message that it's not okay to ask for what you want. Test it yourself. Do you ever ask for what you want right now in your life? Do you tell your spouse, your kids, your colleagues or your friends what you want?

By failing to ask, you limit your potential. What would happen if you took the risk to feel uncomfortable and started asking for what you want? What difference would it make to your intimate relationships, to your career, and to your friendships? Because I'm not (that) afraid to do so, I'm asking you to reclaim your asking power. Start asking for what you want, whether it is borrowing someone else's pen or getting a raise. Remember, when you don't ask the answer is always no.

When you fail to ask, you tell your subconscious you don't really matter and that your preferences and desires are unimportant. As you do so, you make yourself smaller and smaller, which erodes your self-esteem. Asking for what you want is a healthy sign you respect and value yourself. It demonstrates that you hold your space in this world, and you are not afraid to assert yourself. Below are some examples of simple things you can ask:

- Are you cold? Ask if you can raise the room temperature.
- Do you want to change seat in the bus/airplane/train? Ask the staff.
- Loved the dessert? Ask for more.
- Are you looking for a specific item in a store? Ask an employee where you can find it.
- Have a question? Ask!

These small requests may seem unimportant, but they aren't. If you're unable to ask for the simplest things, how will you muster the courage to ask for bigger things that genuinely matter to you? Remember, each time you fail to assert yourself, your self-esteem suffers.

Once you're accustomed to asking for small things, I encourage you to go one step further and ask for more than you believe you can receive. As you do so, you'll realize how much you've been limiting yourself by not daring to ask. Remember, you're not constraining anyone, you're merely asking. It could look like this:

Would you mind if ...

Do you think I could ...

I wanted to know if I could ...

I was wondering whether ...

May I have ...

Asking is a way to open yourself up to new opportunities. It allows you to expand rather than shrink yourself and, as such, it can be perceived as an act of self-respect and self-love.

Here is a new assumption you can adopt:

I allow myself to ask for what I want.

I talk in greater detail about the importance of asking and how you can overcome your fears of asking in my book, *The Passion Manifesto: Escape the Rat Race, Uncover Your Passion and Design a Career and Life You Love.*

Exercise:

Write down the top three things you wanted to ask but didn't. Ask yourself, what if I could ask these things?

Negative assumption #32—I already know that

Together with, "I can't," these four words form one of the most dangerous phrases in the English language. Have you ever been around people who seem to know everything, yet they fail to obtain any tangible results in "real" life? They read all the books on how to create more wealth but are still broke. They know all the theory on how to approach the opposite sex, but never actually do it. They've been to dozens of self-help seminars and read hundreds of books but are still in the same place they were before. They are the ones telling you, "I already know that," while they don't act on their so-called knowledge. They just think they do.

The truth is, most of the things you think you know, you don't. They're merely concepts; you haven't actually put them into practice or made them part of your identity. You can only master something by repeating it enough times to make it ingrained and easy. Only then can you say you know it.

Do you watch videos on how to become a better public speaker but have yet to try any public speaking? Do you believe you know everything about marketing because you went to business school, but haven't actually done any marketing? Then, you don't have real knowledge about these things.

When you believe you already know something, you close yourself off to change and miss opportunities for growth. You dismiss things you read or hear about since "there's nothing new here," and you keep looking for the magic pill that will give you results with minimum effort. However, in reality, you seldom need more knowledge—you already know what to do—you just need to embody what you know intellectually.

In effect, you need to apply what you learn.

Here is a more empowering assumption to adopt:

If I don't live it, I don't know it.

Exercise:

Write down ten things you believe you know but actually don't, (i.e., things you know intellectually but haven't actually applied in your life). The easiest way to do this is to look at results you're after but haven't been able to produce (yet).

Negative assumption #33—I've reached a plateau and can't improve anymore

While you may believe you can't improve at your job anymore or can't further develop any of your current skills, this is seldom, if ever, the case. Hitting a plateau is natural, but you have to remember you can always improve. There is no limit to what you can learn. Through constant self-reflection, repeated effort and continuous learning, you can improve on anything and thereby attain what you want in life. Having an average IQ cannot prevent you from becoming great at what you do. In fact, someone of average intelligence but who is curious, passionate and persistent will, in many cases, outperform a genius in the long term.

Your brain is malleable. You can rewire it and use it to learn anything you want. By using the power of repetition, you can internalize movements, tasks and ways of thinking. Repetition allows you to transfer your learning to your subconscious, making you feel almost as though you have superpowers—and you do. Take driving, for instance. The first time you took the wheel you were likely scared, unsure you would ever be able to drive. Years later, it has become effortless. You can now drive while talking to your friends or listening to music. The same process works for anything else you want to learn. Have you ever wondered why world-class athletes are so obsessed with nailing the fundamentals? This is because they must be able to execute key movements perfectly even under intense pressure. To do so, they must master the fundamentals until it becomes second nature. This is why you'll see world-class performers practicing the same movements over and over again. Basketball players repeat the same shots thousands of times. Tennis players practice their serve for hours. Golfers rehearse their swings over and over.

The bottom line is if you reached a plateau, it means you probably haven't fully integrated the concept of self-reflection, constant improvement and repetition. To progress at anything, you must isolate the key skills and tasks needed to improve your performance and master them by designing specific exercises you can practice consistently. Remember, to become exceptional at what you do, repetition is key. As Bruce Lee said, "*I fear not the man who has practiced ten thousand kicks once, but I fear the man who has practiced one kick ten thousand times.*"

What separates successful people from unsuccessful ones more than anything else is repetition, not IQ.

To learn more, you can refer to the chapters on skills in my books:

Upgrade Yourself: Simple Strategies to Transform Your Mindset, Improve Your Habits and Change Your Life, and

The One Goal: Master the Art of Goal Setting, Win Your Inner Battles and Achieve Exceptional Results.

You can adopt the following assumption:

Everything is learnable, and I can always improve.

Exercise:

Identify an area in which you feel stuck or fail to get the results you want. Ask yourself, what can I do to get unstuck?

6

ASSUMPTIONS ABOUT MONEY

Money is an important topic, and it is essential we spend some time uncovering your assumptions about it. In this section, I'll share with you disempowering assumptions commonly held and help you adopt more empowering ones that will allow you to think of money in a whole different way.

Negative assumption #34—Money is not important

A common assumption is that money is not important. Now, if you hold such an assumption, what are your chances of generating enough money to live in abundance? I would say zero or close to it.

Every time you hear someone saying that money is not important, you can be pretty sure they are broke or at least far from being what you would call wealthy.

Here's the truth people don't want to admit: *money is important.* Otherwise, why would most people trade forty-odd years of their lives to work at a job they hate? Isn't it so that they can pay their rent, put food on the table and send their kids to college? Now, if you had enough money to never have to work again, would you still be working at your current job? If not, I'm afraid money *is* important to you.

It is likely you also spend a lot of time thinking (or worrying) about money, as many people do. If so, saying money is not important is clearly BS. That's like being angry at someone and pretending everything is okay. You may try to convince yourself you don't care but, if in the back of your mind you can't stop thinking about someone or something, you probably do care.

Another way to assess whether money is important to you is by asking yourself, "Would I change my life drastically as a result of having more money in my bank account?" If so, whether you admit it or not, money is important to you.

To design a future where you go to work because you *want* to, not because you *have* to, it is critical you reassess your relationship with money. No, money is not everything. There are many things more valuable, such as time, friendship, love or health. However, accepting money is important is by no means dismissing the value of all these other things. As we discussed previously, it doesn't have to be either one or the other. You can have both. The truth is money can be a powerful enabler and, when used properly, it can do wonderful things.

There is one main reason I believe money is important: money buys time. And time, because of its scarcity, is more valuable than money. This is where most people get it wrong. They treat money as if it were scarce, and they waste their time as though time were abundant. Some surveys show that American adults watch TV five hour per day. If we extrapolate these results, it means people spend on average sixteen years of their lives watching TV. While I do enjoy watching TV from time to time, I'm not willing to waste a quarter of my life sitting on a couch mindlessly watching TV shows. I'd rather spend my life mindfully sitting in front of a screen—my computer—and do something more meaningful (hopefully).

The point is you don't create wealth by treating your time as a commodity. You create wealth by valuing your time more than anything else. If Bill Gates schedules appointments in six-minute increments, there must be a reason for that. Remember, you can double or triple your income, but you cannot double or triple your lifespan.

As a side effect of having more money and/or time, you also have the freedom to do whatever you want to do, whether it is spending time with your family, traveling around the world or doing charity work.

You can adopt the following assumption:

Money is important.

Exercise:

Answer the following questions with brutal honesty:

- If you had enough money to never have to work again, would you still be working at your current job?
- Do you often think about money? (Worrying, fantasizing about making more money etc.) What does this say about your relationship with money?
- Would you change your life drastically as a result of having more money in your bank account? If so, how?

Now, based on your answers, how important is money to you?

Negative assumption #35—Money is the root of all evil

Another common assumption is that money is the root of all evil. The truth is money is simply a tool—a means of exchange. In itself, money is neutral. It is neither bad nor good. When used wisely, it can do great things, when used poorly, it can do harm.

I suspect the reason money may seem like the root of evil, is because it tends to amplify who you already are. If you're generous it can make you more generous, if you're greedy, it can make you even greedier. In short, money gives you more room to express yourself. Thus, rather than seeing money as the root of evil, I encourage you to see it as a method for expressing yourself—in a positive way.

While many people see wealth as anti-religious or anti-spiritual, I've started seeing money as a spiritual thing. First, as Lynne Twist explains in her book, *The Soul of Money*, money can be used as a tool to express yourself. Second, the simple fact of giving yourself permission to accumulate wealth—or give it away—can be seen as a spiritual practice in itself. It requires that you conduct real inner work to remove any limiting beliefs and feeling of unworthiness or scarcity you may currently have. Sadly, many people—especially spiritual people—are afraid to charge for their work because of their beliefs about money. In addition to money being anti-spiritual, some common beliefs include:

- I want to charge more but I don't feel worthy of it.
- I feel as though I'm ripping people off.
- I'm afraid my clients can't afford to pay me that price.

The first thing you need to understand is that it's not your job to decide whether you're worthy of charging a certain price for your products or services. Charge what you think your products or services are worth and let your clients decide. The second thing to understand is that if you don't value yourself and respect yourself, your clients won't either, and you won't be able to make the amount of money you need to survive and thrive. Often, not charging enough can reduce the perceived value of your products and be detrimental to your clients or customers in other ways. Firstly, if they buy another, inferior product or service just because it's more expensive. Secondly, if they buy your product or service but don't use it as effectively because of its perceived low value (cheaper price).

Your ability to receive payment for what you're worth—and hence, your ability to earn more money—is also connected to *your* level of self-esteem. Choosing to create more abundance in your life forces you to face your inner demons and overcome some of your fears and insecurities.

In fact, you may hold many other assumptions about money. Perhaps you believe you shouldn't make more money than your parents. Or you may be afraid your family or friends will reject you if you become rich. You may also assume that making more money means you're stealing other people's wealth. And this is just the tip of the iceberg in terms of the money-related assumptions you may hold.

Part of your personal development journey is to remove all these assumptions and replace them with more empowering ones. Whenever you experience fear, shame or guilt in relation to money, you can be sure that you hold certain disempowering beliefs.

Whenever you have to deal with money, start observing what's going on inside you. How do you feel about investing in yourself? Are you scared of buying an expensive program that could make a big difference in your life? Notice this. What about charging for your products or services? Do you feel bad about doing this? Notice how it feels. Do you find it difficult to give money to charity because you live in scarcity? Take note of this as well.

Remember, whenever you face your fears and move beyond your comfort zone, you open yourself up to new possibilities. This goes for money-related fears as well. Whenever you stretch yourself and invest more in yourself than you feel comfortable doing, you grow. Whenever you give money to charity when you don't have much disposable income, you change your relationship with money and start removing some of your fears. Whenever you face discomfort and decide to charge for your work, you loosen some of your limiting beliefs about money as well. But more importantly, you signal to yourself that you value your work, which boosts your confidence and opens new opportunities for you.

As you can see, money isn't a bad thing, per se. Again, it's simply a matter of perspective. Some people want to make more money out of greed and fear. Instead, I suggest you use money as a way to remove your fears, expand your comfort zone and uncover your potential.

Whenever you witness certain patterns, such as constantly making and losing money, struggling to invest in yourself or always being in debt, look at some of your assumptions about money. In his book, *Secrets of The Millionaire Mind*, T. Harv Ecker explains how everybody has a money blueprint. Your blueprint is often inherited from your parents and tends to be either the same as your parents' blueprint or the exact opposite. See if you can find your own blueprint, whether it is saving a lot, overspending or refusing to charge enough for your work. What can you learn from this and what can you do about it?

You can adopt the following assumption:

I give myself total permission to give and receive money in abundance.

Exercise:

What is one small action you could take to change your relationship with money and extend your comfort zone (e.g., give money to charity, invest in yourself, charge more for your services, etc.)?

Negative assumption #36—Being poor is noble

You may believe being poor is a noble thing and feel good about yourself as a result. However, in reality, being poor in itself doesn't qualify you as a good or noble person. After all, it's the default position and requires no effort, does it? That's not to say there is anything wrong with it, though. There is just nothing fundamentally noble about being poor.

A major problem is that struggling financially doesn't help anybody. On the contrary, it drastically limits your ability to serve others. It is challenging to help others when you're struggling yourself and have little to no access to resources, such as money. You may already be helping many people and that's wonderful, but imagine how many more people you could help with more resources. Perhaps you could serve ten times or even a hundred times more people. Wouldn't that be better for everybody?

I hear you screaming, "But what about Mother Theresa? Wasn't she poor?" The major difference between Mother Theresa and most people struggling financially, is that she was poor by choice not by default. In fact, she was a fantastic fundraiser and raised millions of dollars for the poor, which is one of the main reasons she was able to make such a massive impact on the world. We could argue that if she wanted to, she could have been rich. One thing to understand is by serving a lot of people you often end up attracting money and support. It could be through people donating money, products and services or through companies/government sponsorship.

Now, I would like to ask, are you where you are financially by choice or by default? Do you pretend money is not important while knowing deep down this attitude is BS? In reality, you would probably like to earn more money, right? Nothing wrong with that (providing you acquire it honestly). Again, money is neutral and whether you have plenty or not enough, it doesn't say anything about you.

Also, did you know the real saying is not, "Money is the root of all evil", but, "*The love of money* is the root of all evil." Loving money to gain more power because of greed is a problem. Channeling money to help the world the same way Mother Theresa did, isn't.

Remember, money is simply a vehicle you can use to express yourself. What does money mean to you? How could you change your assumptions about money in a way that leads to positive changes in your life? And how will you use it in a way that is consistent with who you are?

Let me suggest you utilize the following assumption:

The more money I have, the more people I can help.

Exercise:

Spend a few seconds to write down the values you give to money, whatever they may be.

Negative assumption #37—Money is scarce

Do you think money is scarce? While people tend to give more importance to money than to time, in reality, time, due to its real scarcity, is far more precious.

Many people are ready to spend hours to save a few dollars, but wealthy people would rather spend their money to save time. I believe the transition from struggling financially to becoming wealthy begins when you realize time is far more precious than money, not the other way around.

The other day, I heard that at my local supermarket, people were almost fighting to get a discounted chocolate paste. They wanted to save a few bucks. Are these people likely to ever become wealthy?

Rather than trying to save a few bucks here and there, it is important to realize you can always find ways to make more money, but you can never get more time. Each second passed is forever gone. Contrary to what many people tend to believe, money isn't limited. It isn't a pie you need to get a slice of before there isn't any left. If that was the case, wealth creation wouldn't exist, and economic growth wouldn't be possible.

Money was first created in the human mind. This means you, like anybody else, have the ability to create wealth. You have the power to generate new ideas that you can turn into tangible things in the physical world. Because of this ability, the amount of wealth you can create is virtually unlimited. I believe that if people were in a position to utilize a mere five percent more of their potential, they could generate a staggering amount of wealth. In fact, when you look at countries like Japan after the Second World War, it becomes apparent that wealth comes first and foremost from the human mind. Few people would have expected a small group of islands with very few natural resources to become an economic superpower in a mere two decades.

The bottom line is, regardless of your external situation— unemployment rate, inflation, international financial meltdowns —you can create wealth. Ask yourself, "In what way(s) am I limiting myself in terms of the amount of wealth I can create?"

What would happen if you decided to hold the assumption that wealth is unlimited, and you can always create more? What if you see yourself as the very source of wealth? How would that change the way you feel, think and act?

You can adopt the following assumption:

Wealth is unlimited, and I can always create more.

Exercise:

Take a few seconds to meditate on the fact that money isn't something external you need to earn or attract. It comes from within you as one manifestation of wealth.

Negative assumption #38 - Money doesn't grow on trees

Have you ever been told that money doesn't grow on trees? I actually believe money does grow on trees. But for that to happen, you have to plant the right seeds. The most important seed for wealth is your mindset, which is what this book is all about. For instance, if you hold the wrong assumptions, such as, "money doesn't grow on trees" or, "rich people are greedy," you're planting the wrong seeds and money will never grow. After all, why would you want to be rich if you believe rich people are greedy? Why would you want to be one of them? Simply by believing rich people are greedy, you dramatically reduce your chances of becoming wealthy. This is the power of assumptions.

Although this is not the specific topic of this book, you can sow other seeds to grow your money trees. Anything that allows you to leverage your work is a great seed. One obvious example is to utilize the internet, which works 24/7, doesn't require your presence and the products you put on it can be bought all over the world. Take this book as an example. It's available to download from Amazon 24/7. Not only that, but if it is ranked high enough,

Amazon's algorithms will keep promoting it for free. Other seeds are outsourcing and delegating. By outsourcing some of your tasks, you can focus on the higher value tasks you are good at and enjoy doing. This is what valuing your time means. Yet another seed would be working with high-end clients or big corporations. In short, going where the money is. Again, no magic pill here. Wealth creation, like success, requires you to follow a specific process over an extended period of time. Certain things—such as building your own company—facilitate the accumulation of wealth. Other things—such as being an employee—make it very challenging.

If you want to learn more about wealth creation, I highly encourage you to check out MJ DeMarco's book, *The Millionaire Fastlane*, which outlines key principles and explains the mindset you need to adopt if you want to create more wealth.

You can adopt the following assumption:

Wealth creation is inevitable, I just have to sow the right seeds.

Exercise:

Write down twenty ways you could attract more money in your life.

Negative assumption #39—Wealth equals money

When we talk about someone being wealthy, we generally mean he or she has a lot of money in his or her bank account. But money is just one manifestation of wealth. What if wealth has nothing to do with money? What if wealth is not something outside you? Instead of thinking of wealth as something external you have to chase and could lose at any moment, imagine if you saw yourself as the very source of wealth. After all, if you removed all your limiting beliefs about money and had confidence in yourself and in your potential, couldn't you create more wealth? Ultimately, aren't you the source of your own wealth?

By choosing to believe you are the source of wealth, you can stop thinking of money as a limited resource. You will know that, by tapping into your resourcefulness, you can create wealth continuously throughout your life. Isn't that a more empowering belief to hold?

Here is the assumption you can adopt:

I'm the source of wealth, and I have enough resourcefulness to attract any resource I need to create wealth.

Exercise:

How resourceful are you? Write down all the qualities and strengths you have and could rely on to attract the resources you need to create wealth. This could be your motivation, passion, creativity, etc.

7

ASSUMPTIONS ABOUT EMOTIONS

The quality of your emotions largely determines the quality of your life. Imagine if you could better manage your emotions and experience more happiness and peace of mind. What would that do for you?

In this section, we'll discuss common assumptions about emotions, and we will offer new empowering assumptions to give you a new perspective.

Negative assumption #40—I am my emotions

Many people live their lives believing they are their emotions. When they feel anger, they react accordingly by yelling at people or taking reckless actions they may later regret. They're so caught up in their personal stories they fail to realize that emotions are only temporary visitors. The truth is, no matter how depressed, angry or despondent you are today, it doesn't make you less of a person than you were three weeks ago when you were feeling great. No emotions can ever affect the essence of who or what you are in the long term.

Think of the worst things that have ever happened to you. Perhaps you lost your job, or your boyfriend or girlfriend broke up with you. Or maybe you were depressed for months. But even the worse episodes of your life ended and, as time passed, you felt better, right?

Your emotions are little more than costumes you wear for a short while. They are clouds hiding the sun. While clouds will eventually disperse, you—the real you—will remain. Start seeing your emotions as temporary visitors or passing clouds. Don't try to change them or judge them. Avoid identifying with them. Just notice them.

Below, I've listed thirty-one simple coping strategies to deal with negative emotions short-term and long-term. These are from my book, *Master Your Emotions: A Practical Guide to Overcome Negativity and Better Manage Your Feelings.*

1. Short-term solutions

The following techniques will help you manage negative emotions as they arise. Try them out and keep the ones that work for you.

a) Change your emotional state

- Distract yourself: An emotion is only as strong as you allow it to be. Whenever you experience a negative feeling, instead of focusing on it, get busy right away. If you're angry about something, focus on an item on your to-do list. If possible, do something that requires your full attention. When you cross something off your to-do list, the positive energy you create will go a long way towards alleviating your negative emotions.

- Interrupt: Do something silly or unusual to break the pattern. Shout, perform a silly dance or speak in a strange voice.
- Move: Stand up, go for a walk, do push-ups, dance, or use a power posture. By changing your physiology, you can often change the way you feel.
- Listen to music: Listening to your favorite music may improve your emotional state.
- Shout: Talk to yourself with a loud and authoritarian voice and give yourself a pep talk. Use your voice and words to change your emotions.

b) Take action

- Do it anyway: Ignore your feeling(s) and do what you have to do. Mature adults do what they have to do whether they feel like it or not.
- Do something about it: Your behavior indirectly influences your feelings. Ask yourself, "What action can I take in today to change the way I feel?" Then, go do it.

c) Become more aware of your emotions

- Write it down: Take a pen and paper and write down what you worry about, why and what you can do about it. Be as specific as possible.
- Write down what happened: Write down exactly what happened to generate the negative emotion. Don't write down your interpretation of it or the drama you created around it. Simply write down the raw facts. Now ask yourself, in the grand scheme of your life, is it really that big a deal?

- Talk: Have a discussion with a friend. You may be overreacting to the situation and making things worse than they are. Sometimes, all you need is a different perspective.
- Remember a time when you felt good about yourself: This can help you return to the same, positive state and gain a new perspective. Ask yourself the following questions, "How did it feel?" "What was I thinking at the time?" "What was my outlook on life at the time?"
- Let your emotion go: Ask yourself, "Can I let that emotion go?" Then, allow yourself to release it.
- Allow your emotions to exist: Stop trying to resist your emotions or to change them. Allow them to be what they are.
- Embrace your emotions: Feel your emotions without judging them. Become curious about them. What are they exactly at their core?

d) Just relax

- Rest: Take a nap or a break. When tired, you are more likely to experience negative emotions than when properly rested.
- Breathe: Breathe slowly to relax. The way you breathe affects your emotional state. Use breathing techniques to calm yourself, or to give you more energy.
- Relax: Take a few minutes to relax your muscles. Start by relaxing your jaw, the tension around your eyes and the muscles on your face. Your body affects your emotions. As you relax your body, your mind will also relax.
- Thank your problems: Understand they are here for a reason and will serve you in some way.

2. Long-term solutions

The following techniques will help you manage your negative emotions long-term.

a) Analyze your negative emotions

- Identify the story behind your emotions: Take a pen and paper and write down all the reasons you have these emotions in the first place. What assumptions do you hold? How did you interpret what's happened to you? Now, see if you can let go of this particular story.
- Write down your emotions in a journal: Take a few minutes each day to write down how you felt during the day. Look for recurring patterns. Then, use affirmations, visualization, or a relevant exercise to help you overcome these emotions.
- Practice mindfulness: Observe your emotions throughout the day. Meditation will help you do this. Another way is simply to engage in an activity while being fully present. As you do this, observe what's going on in your mind.

b) Move away from negativity

- Change your environment: If you're surrounded by negativity, change your environment. Move to a different place or reduce the time you spend with negative people.
- Remove counterproductive activities: Remove or reduce the time you spend on any activity that doesn't have a positive impact on your life. This could be reducing the time you spend watching TV or surfing the internet.

c) Condition your mind

- Create daily rituals: This will help you to experience more positive emotions. Meditate, exercise, repeat positive affirmations, create a gratitude journal and so on. (The best time to deposit positive thoughts in your mind is right before going to sleep and first thing in the morning.)
- Exercise: Exercise regularly. Exercise improves your mood and is good for your emotional and physical health.

d) Increase your energy

- The less energy you have, the more likely you are to experience negative emotions.
- Make sure you get enough sleep: If possible, go to bed and wake up at the same time every day.
- Eat healthier food: As the saying goes, "You are what you eat." Junk food will negatively impact your energy levels, so take steps to improve your diet.
- Rest: Take regular naps or take a few minutes to relax.
- Breathe: Learn to breathe properly.

e) Ask for help

- Consult a professional: if you have deep emotional issues such as extreme low self-esteem or chronic depression, it might be wise to consult a professional.

You can adopt the following assumptions:

Emotions come and go. What I am, remains untouched forever.

To learn more about how to master your emotions, I highly encourage you to refer to my book, *Master Your Emotions: A Practical Guide to Overcome Negativity and Better Manage Your Feelings.*

Exercise:

Remember one of the worst things that ever happened to you. Now, notice how it has passed.

Negative assumption #41—My emotions dictate my actions

Have you noticed that the way you feel usually influences your actions? For instance, when you're angry, you may yell at someone or leave the room. Thus, it sounds reasonable to assume your emotions dictate your actions. However, in reality, *you* dictate your actions, not your emotions. You have the power to act despite your emotions. For instance:

* Being afraid of something doesn't mean you cannot do it.
* Being tired doesn't mean you can't work on your side business.
* Believing you can't do something doesn't mean you are actually unable to do it.

In short, you don't need to feel like it to do something. In fact, one of the major differences between successful people and others is that they do what they need to do whether they feel like it or not.

The idea you must feel like it to do something is a myth. That's why it's so important to rely on processes—a set of tasks you perform daily—to stay on track with your long-term goals. Processes allow you to remain consistent, regardless of what happens to you in the short term and how you feel inside. If you can install and follow processes, you can achieve anything you want.

You can adopt the following assumption:

I dictate my actions, regardless of the way I feel.

Exercise:

Knowing you dictate your actions, not your emotions, what will you start doing differently from now? What will you do whether you feel like it or not?

Negative assumption #42—I get upset because of something external

Another major assumption is that you become upset because something happens to you. The real reason you get upset is *not* because of what is actually happening, it's because of your *interpretation* of what is happening. Fundamentally, nothing can upset you. Let me give you an example:

Let's say you're about to leave for a picnic and it starts raining. You're now angry at the rain. But is it the rain that's the problem or is it the meaning you assign to it? While you're complaining about the rain, could it be that farmers somewhere are rejoicing?

Now, how would your life change if every time you get upset, you look at the meaning you give to the event rather than blaming external factors?

I recommend you use the following assumption:

Nothing outside me has the power to upset me.

Exercise:

Select something that upset you recently. Look at what happened objectively without adding your interpretation to the event. Notice how the issue probably isn't the event itself, but the story you've attached to it.

Negative assumption #43—I'm responsible for how other people feel

It's not your job to make other people feel good. I'm not saying you shouldn't be nice. I'm saying that you're not responsible for how other people feel. It's *their* job to control their emotions, *not* yours. In what world would we be living if we had to constantly watch our words lest we offend someone?

I believe that being offended is part of our personal growth. It's what allows us to remove our excessive attachment to our false sense of identity. It enables us to stop clinging so much to our physical attributes or beliefs about ourselves and the world.

I explain in more details how you can use feelings of defensiveness as a tool for your personal growth in my book, *Master Your Emotions: A Practical Guide to Overcome Negativity and Better Manage Your Feelings*.

Some people are easily offended, while others remain unaffected no matter what happens. This demonstrates it's not what you say that hurts people, it's their inability to deal with their emotions. Feelings of defensiveness are, in fact, incredible tools to help identify what you need to work on to become a more self-assured human being. Are you offended by comments people make about your body, the way you walk, or the way you talk? If so, what does it say about the relationship you have with yourself? What do you need to work on to avoid feeling the need to defend yourself? Or perhaps you're offended when someone criticizes some of your beliefs. It could be political or religious beliefs, or it could be beliefs about yourself. Remember, you are responsible for your emotional state. Similarly, other people are responsible for the way they feel.

Having said that, I don't recommend offending people on purpose, but I do encourage you to internalize the fact that, ultimately, you are not responsible for people's emotions. *They* are.

You can adopt the following assumption:

I'm responsible for how I feel, not for how other people feel.

Exercise:

Identify one situation where worrying about how others may feel prevents you from doing something you really want to do.

Negative assumption #44—Complaining is natural

Most people tend to believe that complaining is normal. Something bad happens to you, so you should complain, right? In reality, complaining is usually ineffective and doesn't help you create the life you want. If anything, it robs you of your power to make changes. I believe complaining is a habit and can be changed with practice.

Interestingly, when we complain about something or someone, we seldom complain about it to the right person—the person who can actually do something about it. When you're angry at your boss, you complain about it to your spouse, your colleagues or your friends. Yet, the best way to improve the situation is probably to talk to your boss directly.

One of the main reasons we complain is to avoid taking responsibility. Complaining is the easiest way out because it allows us to do nothing to improve the situation—nothing but complain. Many people complain about their current situation, saying they want to be somewhere else, do something else or become someone else, yet they do nothing about it. If you look at any situation in your life, you'll see that you only have three options:

- Complain
- Proactively do something to address/improve the situation, or
- Accept the situation.

Unfortunately, complaining isn't often a viable strategy which leaves you with two options:

- Do something about the situation.
- Accept the situation as it is.

Let me give you some examples:

Example 1: You're complaining because you believe you're not getting paid enough at work. You can:

- Keep complaining (but does that help you solve the problem?).
- Do something about it (ask for a raise, work overtime, change your job, start a side business etc.).
- Accept your current income without complaining.

Now, which option do you think is the easiest one? Complaining, of course. Most people choose the easiest path. But remember what the motivational speaker Les Brown said, *"Do what is easy, and your life will be hard. Do what is hard, and your life becomes easy."*

I wish everybody could earn ten times their current income, but that's not how reality works. As the motivational speaker, Jim Rohn, said, *"You can't get rich by demand."*

You can go on strike and complain as much as you want, but you're not going to double or triple your salary. Unless you have the power to change the entire economic system, your only choice is to take full responsibility for your life and make decisions that will allow you to make the amount of money you want to make. There is no point complaining, because the economic system is not answering your personal wishes.

Example 2: You're complaining because you're paying too much tax. You can:

- Keep complaining.
- Do something about it (find ways to pay fewer taxes, move to another country with more liberal tax laws, etc.).
- Accept your situation (and happily pay your taxes).

Example 3: You're complaining because you don't like your current life. You can:

- Keep complaining (and nothing will change).
- Do something about it (ask for advice, design your ideal life and take action etc.).
- Accept your current situation.

In short, complaining keeps you in a "victim mentality." In any situation, you can either do something about it or accept things as they are. Anything else—such as complaining—is not only ineffectual, it is insanity.

Your assumption:

Instead of complaining, I either do something about my situation or fully accept it.

Exercise:

For one full day, refuse to complain about anything. If you want, you can extend this challenge for as long as you like. A great book to read on the topic is Will Bowen's, *A Complaint Free World: How to Stop Complaining and Start Enjoying the Life You Always Wanted.*

8

———

ASSUMPTIONS ABOUT WORK

You'll spend a large part of your life working. Now, would you rather do something you enjoy or something you hate? Unfortunately, people often hold limiting beliefs that prevent them from having the fulfilling career they love. In this section, we'll challenge a few common assumptions that could stop you designing your ideal career.

Negative assumption #45—I can't find a job I love

Do you dread Monday mornings and celebrate Friday afternoons as though you were a kid on Christmas Day? One day, my supervisor told me we didn't have to love our job. He thought a job was merely a way to earn a living. I almost believed him, but something didn't seem quite right to me so I didn't. Now, can you imagine what would have happened if I had listened to him and believed I couldn't find a job I love? For a start, I wouldn't have written this book!

What about you? Do you believe you're not supposed to enjoy your job? Do you find it acceptable to hang around for years at the same job because people told you this is the way it has to be?

What if you replace your assumption, "*I can't find a job that I love,*" with "*I can find (or create) a job I love. And I will!*" What effect will this, apparently minor, revision have on your life? What will you start doing differently today?

Adopt the following assumption:

I can find a job I love, and I will!

To learn how to find what you love and make a career out of it, refer to my book, The Passion Manifesto: Escape The Rat Race, Uncover Your Passion and Design a Career and Life You Love.

Exercise: What does your ideal job look like? Write it down.

Negative assumption #46—I can't make money doing what I love

Do you believe it's impossible to make money doing what you love? If so, how likely are you to ever work at a job you actually enjoy?

It is *absolutely* possible to make money doing something you love. In fact, millions of people enjoy their job—though they sometime have to do it secretly to avoid annoying the majority of people who hate what they have to do to earn a living.

I'm not saying finding the perfect job is easy, but I am saying it is possible. And if you're willing to do what it takes, you *will* eventually find a satisfying job. Millions of people have done this before you and so can you. There is no doubt about it.

Now, what if you hold the following assumption:

I can absolutely make money doing what I love.

Exercise:

Write down twenty ideas on how you could make money doing what you love.

Negative assumption #47—I have to work forty plus years and retire at sixty-five

The common view is that we're supposed to work forty plus years, eight hours (or more) per day until we can finally retire at sixty-five. This assumption often remains unchallenged, but is it the only option? What if you want to take a long break, work less or retire early? It is important you stretch your thinking and consider other possibilities that may better suit you. There is no rule that says you have to work from 9 to 5, five days a week. The eight-hour day was originally designed for factory workers who would work in shifts. In many cases, it is not the most productive way to work.

In today's world, the possibilities are limitless. You can decide how you want to work. The key is to have clarity. The more you know what you want, the easier it will be to design your ideal career. While vague goals lead to vague results, crystal-clear goals create extraordinary results.

Your assumption could be:

I have the power to design my career the way I want to.

Exercise:

Where would you like to be professionally in five years? Write down what your ideal career would look like.

Negative assumption #48—I work hard now so I can enjoy my life once I finally retire

Many people are willing to endure years at jobs they hate in exchange for a reward called "retirement." This is a completely terrible idea.

First, there is no guarantee you will live long enough to retire. Many people die before they reach their sixties. Second, at sixty-five you might not be as healthy as you imagine. You might even be unable to do all the wonderful things you planned for your retirement. This is what many people discover when they retire. Third, believing you'll be living happily ever after can lead you to make wrong career choices. You may work hard trying to make money to find yourself sick or depressed at sixty-five.

A wonderful question I encourage you to ask yourself right now is: "Assuming I could never retire and had to work until the day I die, would I still be doing what I'm currently doing?" If not, you might need to change something. The good news is that you now have new powerful assumptions to support you:

1) *I can find a job I love. And I will!*

2) *I can absolutely make money doing what I love.*

3) *I have the power to design my career the way I want to.*

Rather than assuming you will retire one day, I suggest you live your life as if retirement wasn't an option. It doesn't mean you should spend all your money recklessly not saving for your old age; it simply means you must find a job or career you don't want to escape or retire from.

You can adopt the following assumption:

I proactively design a career I love, and I enjoy life now.

Exercise:

Answer the following question, "Assuming I could never retire and had to work until the day I die, would I still be doing what I'm currently doing?"

9

ASSUMPTION ABOUT TIME

Time is one of the most important resources we have. In this section, we'll cover two major assumptions that could prevent you from making the most of your time.

Negative assumption #49—I don't have enough time

Do you struggle to find time to do the things you want to do? We all have twenty-four hours each day. Some people use their time to achieve all their goals and dreams, sometimes they even exceed their expectations. These individuals often accomplish more in one year than most people do in ten. Others stay at the same place all their lives not achieving any of their dreams.

For most people, the issue is not lack of time, but lack of priority and clarity. People who achieve their goals know exactly what they want and work on making it a reality every single day. These individuals have a vision for their lives and make sure what they do every day is aligned with their long-term vision. They are proactive.

Other people are reactive. They wake up every day without having a clear vision of what they want to accomplish by the end of the day, let alone the end of the year. As a result, they waste time on activities that contribute nothing to the life they aspire for. They engage in gossiping, waste hours in front of the TV or spend much of their time on unproductive tasks.

In reality, you *do* have time.

What if you ditch the excuse "I don't have time," for the following assumption:

I make the time to do whatever I'm committed to

Did you notice the word "committed" there? Committing presupposes that you know exactly what you want (clarity) and you resolve to make it happen (priority). These two components are essential to ensure you use your time effectively. So, decide what you want, and make it an absolute priority in your life.

Your assumption therefore is:

I make the time to do whatever I'm committed to.

Exercise:

For an entire week, write down every activity you do at work and at home. Now, look at all your tasks. Which ones are really productive? Do you really not have time to strive for your goal in life?

Negative assumption #50—Money is more valuable than time

While most people treat money as if it were more important than time, we've seen it is not the case. *Time is way more precious than money.* It is one of the scarcest resources you have. Dying billionaires would probably give away all their money to live a few more days, wouldn't they?

Sadly, many people manage their time extremely poorly. They give it away as if it were free and abundant. In many regards, they behave as if they had an infinite amount of time. They happily offer their time to anybody who asks for it. Some will even wait hours in line to save a few bucks.

Other people may expect you to give your time freely—because they do so themselves—but that does not mean you should. You must protect your time and use it wisely. Whether you're asked to join a cause, organize an event, or take on an extra project at work, be willing to say no when it doesn't align with your values and vision. Remember, once time is gone, it's gone forever.

The reason people waste so much time is because they don't have a clear sense of direction and, thus, they have no priorities. In some cases, they don't even know what spending their time efficiently would look like. In short, they have no clear vision for their lives. And people who have no vision can often end up helping other people—who do have one—achieve it. Is that what you want? Are you giving your time to other people to help them live a great life? Or would you rather spend your time strategically and design *your* ideal life?

A great question I like to ask myself is, "If I keep doing what I'm doing today, will I end up where I want to be in ten years from now?" This is a fantastic way to check whether you're using your time wisely or wasting it. Try it.

The bottom line is that, to succeed in life, having a long-term vision is *essential*. You don't build a house without a clear blueprint first, do you? No. You create a detailed plan. You must do the same with your life. You must see a decade or two—or even longer—into your future and decide how you want your life to be. Then, once you have a crystal-clear vision, you can determine what you need to do today, this week, this month and this year to move closer to that ideal vision.

Now, you might think I'm asking you to time everything you do to the second and avoid wasting time at all cost. No, I'm not asking you to drink less water, so you can go to the bathroom less often to save a few minutes. I'm not saying you shouldn't spend hours chatting with friends either. What I'm suggesting is you start using your time more deliberately.

While people tend to believe that productivity is about producing more in less time, I believe the real meaning of productivity is to spend most of your time doing what you want to do, whether it is working a job you're passionate about, meeting your friends or spending time with your family. You can be the most productive person in your company, but if you spend seventy hours a week at a job you hate until the day you retire, that's not what I call being productive. It might be productive for your company, but not for you or your family.

Successful people value time more than money and, as a result, they can create more money if they choose to. They use their money to save time, not their time to save money. Start thinking and acting like them. Value your time more! By doing so, you'll develop more self-respect, become more productive and, as a result, you will create more freedom in your life.

Your new assumption:

I value my time because I value myself.

Exercise:

Write down all the tasks you could stop doing because they aren't aligned with your vision or aren't productive.

To learn more about productivity, I encourage you to refer to my book, *Productivity Beast, An Unconventional Guide to Getting Things Done.*

PART III

CREATING NEW ASSUMPTIONS

Now we've reviewed and torn apart common assumptions, it is time to look specifically at your assumptions and make sure you replace them with more empowering ones.

You may be familiar with the concepts of affirmation and visualization, but we're going to go one step further here. We don't merely want to repeat some affirmations, we want to have a look at your current web of beliefs, or "life assumptions," and replace them with more empowering beliefs, ones that will allow you to design the life you want. We want to create your "Identity Map 2.0."

The sum of all your assumptions forms your programming, that is, how you think, feel and act. And, since your Identity Map determines the actions you take, it determines the results you obtain.

- If you believe rich people are greedy, you'll never become wealthy yourself.
- If you believe you're not good enough or can't do something, you'll give up prematurely.
- If you believe you're a dunce, like Victor Serebriakoff did, you may give up on yourself.
- If you believe success is an event rather than a process that includes countless "failures," you will never achieve your most exciting goals and dreams.
- If you believe your emotions dictate your actions, you won't discipline yourself enough to do the necessary work to achieve the results you desire.
- If you believe it's normal to hate your job, you probably won't do what it takes to design a career you love.

We all have different assumptions. Among the assumptions we discussed previously, you may have found new empowering assumptions you can't wait to adopt in your life. You may also decide not to adopt some others, and this is perfectly fine.

The most important thing is for you to start selecting the most empowering assumptions, ones that will support you in creating the kind of life you dream of living.

10

MOVING FROM WHO YOU ARE TO WHO
YOU WANT TO BE

In this section, we're going to craft your Identity Map 2.0 by adopting new empowering assumptions that will help you change your life. We will remove weeds from your garden and sow powerful new seeds that will transform your life.

Imagine how your life would change if you could remove, one by one, all the limiting beliefs that have been destroying your potential and, instead, implement powerful beliefs that will serve you for the rest of your life.

While most people react to life based on the unconscious assumptions they hold, I want you to select empowering assumptions that strongly resonate within you and implement them in your life. These empowering assumptions will become the core beliefs that dictate your actions and shape your destiny.

Selecting your core life assumptions

Let's start by unearthing your major assumptions about life.

We introduced the following assumptions earlier:

- *Life is easy. And I do whatever I can to keep it this way.*
- *I'm as happy as anybody else.*
- *As I change, my environment changes.*
- *I create my own reality. What others believe I can or cannot do is irrelevant.*
- *By giving more, I open myself to receiving more.*
- *Having problems is normal. The less attached I am to them, the more irrelevant they become.*
- *In any problem lies opportunity.*
- *I fully accept what is, and I can create what will be.*
- *Every day I start anew, free of any burden from the past.*
- *I'm good enough for now.*
- *I'm perfect in my imperfections.*
- *My intent is pure.*
- *I matter.*
- *I believe it, and therefore I'll see it.*
- *Because I start before I'm ready, I can achieve anything I want faster than I ever thought possible.*
- *I ask for whatever I want, regardless of how I feel.*
- *I'm the scriptwriter of my life, and I can rewrite my story at will.*
- *I'm motivated because I have a motive for action.*
- *Self-discipline equals freedom. With enough self-discipline, I can achieve anything I want.*
- *I take care of me for my family and friends.*
- *I'm never too old to do what I want to do.*
- *I help others and myself grow by telling the truth whenever possible.*

To begin with, select only five assumptions from this list. If you were to adopt them, what five assumptions would make the biggest difference in your life?

Selecting assumptions in major areas of your life

Now you have selected your top five life assumptions, let's look at some major assumptions you could adopt in various areas of your life.

Below is a summary of the assumptions we introduced previously:

Success

- *Success is inevitable.*
- *Success is not about what I have, it's about who I become.*
- *I happily fail my way to success. I fail faster and better each time.*
- *I'm successful because I'm making progress toward my goal.*
- *I create my own success regardless of external circumstances.*
- *I'm already there, and I'm more than enough for now.*
- *By having changed some people's lives, even in a minor way, I'm already a huge success.*
- *I have good intentions, therefore I'm a massive success.*
- *Food + shelter = happiness + success.*
- *I can have it all.*
- *I allow myself to ask for what I want.*
- *If I don't live it, I don't know it.*
- *Everything is learnable, and I can always improve.*

Money

- *Money is important.*
- *I give myself total permission to give and receive money in abundance.*
- *The more money I have, the more people I can help.*

- *Wealth is unlimited, and I can always create more of it.*
- *Wealth creation is inevitable, I just have to plant the right seeds.*
- *I'm the source of wealth. I have enough resourcefulness to attract any resources I need to create wealth.*

Emotions

- *Emotions come and go. What I am, remains untouched. Forever.*
- *I dictate my actions, regardless of the way I feel.*
- *Nothing outside of me has the power to upset me.*
- *I'm responsible for how I feel, not for how other people feel.*
- *I refuse to complain. I do something about it or I accept it.*

Work

- *I can find a job I love, and I will!*
- *I can absolutely make money doing what I love.*
- *I have the power to design my career the way I want to.*
- *I proactively design a career I love and enjoy my life now.*

Time

- *I make the time to do whatever I'm committed to doing.*
- *I value my time because I value myself.*

Now, let's see how you can start creating a new identity by using some of these empowering assumptions.

11

CREATING YOUR IDENTITY MAP

You become what you believe. No matter where you are now in life, you can change your environment by changing your beliefs. You can create a brand new identity and become more confident, determined, motivated and powerful than you can ever imagine. Remember, you already have everything you need to achieve anything you want. You just have to remove the filters preventing you from shining.

Whatever disempowering assumptions you hold, you can remove.

Whatever fears you have, you can overcome.

Whatever habits or skills you need, you can develop.

It's now time to rewire your brain and create a new identity that will allow you to obtain the results you want in life. We'll create your Identity Map 2.0 using your free action guide here. Alternatively, you can use a separate sheet of paper.

In the middle, write down, "My best self." Then, create branches for each area in which you want to implement new empowering assumptions. I recommend you use the same categories we use in this book. Feel free to add, remove or alter categories to fit your personal needs. Remember, this is all about *you* and the life you want to create for *yourself*.

Start with the questions: "Who do I want to become? If I were to adopt them, what new empowering assumptions would allow me to be that person? "

Strengthening your new identity

Now you've created your Identity Map, you can start adopting the new empowering assumptions you've selected. You can use two things to rewire your brain: repetition and emotion. By having the same thought over and over again and charging it emotionally, you create new neural connections for that specific thought pattern and, by doing so, you strengthen it. You physically change your brain! Remember, your brain is malleable. You can create new neural connections and implement/remove any belief you desire. And you can do so, whether you're fifteen or seventy years old.

How to change your identity

To make your new assumptions part of yourself, you must focus on them as often as possible. Dedicate time each day to repeating them. I recommend you spend five minutes each morning when you wake up and five minutes each evening before falling asleep. Make your assumptions the first thing you think of in the morning and the last thing you think of at night, which is when your subconscious mind is at its most receptive.

At first, refer to your mind map and repeat each assumption you've written aloud. Repeat them multiple times. As you do so, try to associate images with your assumptions. If your assumption is "success is inevitable," envision what success means to you. What specific goal or vision will you inevitably achieve? Can you visualize specific situations? Perhaps you are standing in front of a large audience, delivering a speech with ease and confidence. Or maybe you're traveling the world. Whatever your vision of success might be, envision as many relevant situations as possible.

Coming up with additional reasons

The next step is to ask yourself why your assumption is true. As an example, let's use: "Success is inevitable."

By coming up with more and more reasons your assumption is true, you reinforce it and make it easier to believe in. Below are some examples of answers.

Success is inevitable for me because:

- I have an incredible ability to learn.
- There is no limit to how much I can grow.
- I have access to all the information in the world.
- I will never give up.
- Other people have done it before, and so can I.
- I'm willing to work hard on myself.
- 7.5 billion people on earth are willing to help me.
- My mind is more powerful than I can ever begin to imagine.
- I'm committed to doing whatever it takes to achieve my goals.

Using anchoring to energize your assumptions

Engage your emotions. Now you know success is inevitable, how does this make you feel? Are you filled with joy, excitement, confidence? Are you proud of yourself? Feel all these emotions. Mix them together.

Then, ask yourself how you can amplify these emotions. You can engage your body and talk out loud to create what the world-famous coach, Tony Robbins, calls, "incantations."

Additional tip:

Listen to music and/or watch videos to help you. Select music/videos that match the belief you want create. You could select motivational videos that give you a sense of confidence or beautiful songs that evoke feelings of gratitude in you. Use whatever works for you.

Linking your assumptions to concrete actions

Your beliefs influence the way you feel and the actions you take. As you change your belief system by adopting new assumptions, the action you take will also change. To begin the process, imagine what some of your actions would be. Make sure they are as specific as possible. Your subconscious loves clarity. Consider the following reasons and add specific examples relevant to your situation.

Success is inevitable therefore:

- I enjoy the process and stay confident no matter what (define the process, which could be specific habits you do every day such as writing, eating a certain type of food or working out).
- I move toward my goal with absolute certainty (state your goal).
- I see "failures" as the feedback I can use to adjust my plan (identify potential failures).

- Nobody can talk me out of my vision (mention specific people who may be holding you back).

Creating reminders

Now you have your Identity Map, put it somewhere you can see it every day. I recommend you put it on your wall, on your desk and/or in a notebook you carry with you. When it comes to adopting new assumptions, repetition and daily exposure is key.

Remember, your mind is very similar to software—you have the power to reprogram it to achieve the results you want.

To ingrain your new assumptions further into your mind, write your assumptions on flashcards. Read your flashcards multiple times every day. This will remind you to feel and behave in accordance with your new assumptions. You can read them at home, during your daily commute or when you go to the bathroom.

Your thirty-day challenge

If you don't live it, you don't know it. Dedicate the next thirty days to implementing new and empowering assumptions. Go through the process described above every single day. Aim to spend at least ten minutes focusing on your new assumptions (five minutes in the morning and five minutes in the evening). Whenever you have free time during the day, think of your assumptions. A good time to do so is when you're taking a shower or commuting.

Additional tips:

Another great way to make your new assumptions part of your identity is to do the thirty-day challenge with your partner or a friend. By doing so, you can validate each other's assumptions—and have fun doing it.

Let's see how you can do the exercise. For example's sake, let's use the assumption, "Success is inevitable."

Step #1 - Say your assumption aloud. *Success is inevitable.*

Step #2 - Have your partner/friend ask why. Make sure you repeat the original assumption to strengthen it. Ask the question three to five times. *Why success is inevitable for you?*

Step #3 - Have your partner/friend ask you to describe in detail what it means. *What exactly does "success is inevitable" mean to you?*

Step #4 – Have your partner/friend ask how you feel about it. *Knowing success is inevitable for you, how does it make you feel? How can you amplify the feeling?*

Personalize your Identity Map

By now, you should have an Identity Map with all your amazing assumptions. Feel free to personalize it. You can add pictures and color to it.

Overcoming fear

As you create your new identity and write down empowering assumptions, you may experience some internal resistance. If so, this means you have some fears and self-doubt about certain assumptions. This is normal. The first step toward overcoming these fears is to notice the resistance. Usually, it manifests somewhere in your body. When you feel resistance, ask yourself where exactly you feel it in your body. Is it in your neck? Is it in your stomach? In your chest?

Once you've located the feeling, observe it. Don't judge it. Don't try to make it go away. Don't try to run away from it. Instead, stay with it. Now ask yourself, where is the most intense part of this feeling?

Focus on this part to the best of your abilities. Again, don't judge it. Be present with it. Send love to it. It's not your enemy. Keep focusing on it until the feeling becomes less and less intense. If the feeling moves to another part of your body, repeat the same process.

Note that you may need to go through the same process several times until the fear dissolves. Then, repeat your assumption one more time and see if the fear is still there. By now, the negative emotion should be less intense and, if you keep practicing this exercise, the fear will eventually dissipate.

This process will work for any fear you may have. It could be fears around money or it could be fear of not being good enough. As you repeat your assumptions every day, be mindful and, whenever you feel resistance, deal with it using the above exercise.

Step-by-step method to creating your new identity

Below is a summary of the step-by-step method you can use to create your new identity.

- Create an Identity Map

- Select your core life assumptions.
- Select assumptions in each area of your life.

- Repeat your assumptions each day for at least ten minutes (five minutes in the morning, five minutes in the evening). Follow the process below:

- Repeat your assumptions (in your mind or out loud).
- Ask yourself why it is true.
- Energize your assumptions by engaging your emotions.
- Envision the concrete actions you can take.

- **Check how you feel.** If you feel resistance, work through it.

- Identify where you feel the emotion in your body.
- Stay present with it until it starts dissolving. Focus on the most intense part of the emotion.
- Repeat this process as many times as necessary for the fear to dissipate.

- **Create reminders**

- Put your mind map on your wall, desk and/or in a notebook you carry with you.
- Write down your assumptions on flashcards and review them several times each day.

12

ASKING "WHAT IF?"

To gain new perspectives, you must create thoughts that never crossed your mind before—thoughts that are so big they scare you, so far out of your current model of reality you have a hard time conceiving them.

The truth is you limit yourself in many ways. There may be things you can't do yet. But if you really wanted to, you could probably do most of them. For instance, you may believe you can't speak in front of a large audience, approach someone to initiate a new relationship or change careers. But all these things are possible.

In this section, I invite you to entertain the idea that some of the things you can only envision in your wildest dreams *are* possible. To do so, I'm going to introduce you to two magical words that will open an entire new world of opportunity. These two words are:

"What if?"

I love these two words because they are reassuring and inviting.

What if you could speak in front of a large audience? *What if* you could approach people in the street? *What if* you could change your career? Maybe it doesn't seem possible to you right now, but just entertain the idea that it could be possible. So, *what if*?

An effective way to stretch yourself beyond your comfort zone is to look at each of the following areas of your life and ask yourself, *"What if?"*

- Career
- Family/friends
- Finance
- Health/fitness
- Relationship
- Personal growth

Answer the following questions:

Career

What if I could have the perfect career?

Family/friends

What if I could experience and share more joy than I ever have with my family and friends?

Finance

What if I could double my income by the end of the year?

Health/fitness

What if I could have lots of energy and feel great every day?

Personal growth

What if I could overcome my fears and grow beyond my imagination?

Relationship

What if I could take my relationship to a whole new level?

Visualize what your life would look like in each of the above situations.

Going beyond your realm of possibility

Did you complete the previous exercise? If so, how did it make you feel?

Now, when you answered the previous questions, you were probably still limiting yourself. Let's think bigger. Let's go over each area one more time and do it for real. I'll provide you with some possible questions, but I want you to come up with your own. Entertain ideas that make you feel really uncomfortable and maybe even a little scared.

Whatever goals you had until now, multiply them by two, then by two again. Then, double or even triple that. Do this until you feel uncomfortable and scared. Dare to explore possibilities you've never thought of before. See if you can stretch yourself and start believing you can make the impossible, possible.

Career

What if I could have the perfect career in exactly the way I want it?

What if I could change my career within twelve months? Six months? One month?

What if I could change my career this week?

Family/friends

What if I could experience ridiculous levels of bliss and joy in the presence of my family and friends? What if I could feel total gratitude for every person who ever showed up in my life?

Finance

What if I could double my income within a year? Within six months? Within thirty days?

What if I could generate ten times my income within a year?

Health/fitness

What if the level of joy I've experienced so far is just a fraction of the level my real self can experience?

What if I could experience intense feelings of bliss as never before?

Personal growth

What if I'm currently just a tiny fraction of the person I could be?

What if I'm just scratching the surface of what is possible for me in this world?

What if I could remove any fear, self-doubt and limitations in any areas of my life and move freely in this world?

Relationship

What if I could take my relationship to a whole new level and one I didn't even know existed?

Committing to the impossible

Let's take this exercise one step further. For each area, ask yourself, "If I had to achieve this crazy vision, what would I do?"

How could you increase your income tenfold within a year? How could you change your career within six months? How could you experience more joy than you ever had before?

Play along and imagine you had to achieve your goals at all cost. Force yourself to think in a way you've never thought before. For the sake of this exercise, stretch yourself as much as you can. The point is not necessarily to achieve all these huge goals but to start moving beyond the limitations you've set for yourself through the assumptions you hold.

If you've completed this exercise, you should have experienced fears and discomfort, which is normal. To achieve a new goal, you have to move from Identity A, the person you are now, to Identity B, the person you need to become to achieve that goal. This entails changing your current assumptions and replacing them with more empowering ones.

A great question to ask yourself when working toward a stretch goal is, "What do I need to believe to achieve this goal?" Answering this question will allow you to discover the new beliefs (assumptions) you can implement to achieve that goal.

Putting things together

One of my main assumptions is that everything is possible. I refuse as much as I can to limit myself or to put other people into small boxes. I believe holding space for anything to happen is extremely important. This is because I understand whatever you think you can't do, you can't. As soon as you judge something as impossible, you exclude it from your field of potentialities. That is, you add an artificial filter and, by doing so, you limit your potential.

Why not assume everything is possible? Can you change the entire world? Maybe. Can you heal yourself? Why not? Is it possible to end wars and end poverty? Perhaps.

In fact, when you look at history, people who ended up changing the world were visionaries who saw things that people believed impossible. If people from the past were to look at today's technologies such as the internet, smartphones or airplanes, how do you think they would react? They would look at these things in disbelief.

Thus, I encourage you to adopt the ultimate assumption: "Everything is possible."

- Can you design your dream career? Yes, everything is possible.
- Can you attract your ideal partner? Yes, everything is possible.
- Can you impact the lives of millions of people around the world? Yes, everything is possible.
- Can you overcome your deepest fears or traumas and live in peace? Yes, everything is possible.

As the famous coach, Tony Robbins, says, "The quality of your questions determines the quality of your life."

As you hold the space for what is possible, I encourage you to keep the following words: "What if?" "Why not?" and "How?"

Below is an example of how you can use these magical worlds:

- What if? What if I could design an amazing career that I love?
- Why not? Why not design a great career I enjoy?
- How? How can I create an exciting career?

Remember: Life is easy, and everything is possible. Success is inevitable. Wealth is unlimited. You can have it all. You can create your own reality and start every day anew, free of any burden from the past. By changing yourself, you can transform your environment. By disciplining yourself, you can achieve anything you want. Nothing can upset you. You're good enough for now. And these are just a small sample of the beliefs you can develop.

I would like to remind you, nothing changes until you do. And more importantly, nothing changes until you take action. For your new assumptions to become part of who you are and allow you to achieve more than you ever thought possible, you *must* take action. While it is true your beliefs largely dictate your actions, it is also true your actions strengthen your beliefs.

A great example is confidence. The more you take baby steps toward your goals and stay consistent long term, the more you build confidence. As you attain more and more goals, you feel better about yourself. You start respecting yourself more, and you will develop a deeper sense of self-trust. You weren't born lacking confidence. Low self-confidence is a result of social conditioning. Or put it differently, low self-confidence is nothing more than an idea in your mind, an assumption you unconsciously adopted. It is by no means who you are. In the same way, you're not shy, you're not lazy or "not good enough."

Another main reason taking action is so important is because it expands your field of possibility. Remember, action cures fear. It cures the false assumptions and the wrong ideas you have about yourself. Your lack of confidence or shyness doesn't stand the test of truth. Action destroys the person you think you are and enables you to reveal who you really are. As the saying goes, everything is hard before it's easy. Many things are outside your comfort zone until they become part of it. The same way driving was once challenging but became effortless, one day public speaking, talking to strangers or anything else you're afraid of can be within your comfort zone.

CONCLUSION

I would like to congratulate you for reading this book until the end. This shows your desire to improve your life and design a brighter and more exciting future.

My sincere hope is the information within this book allows you to shift your perspective and open yourself to new possibilities. You have an almost limitless potential and you can make an infinite number of choices every day. Refuse to confine yourself and refuse to make yourself smaller than you are. Instead, hold the space for more, and see yourself as you could be, rather than as you believe yourself to be right now. Whenever you catch yourself saying, "I can't do this or that," take a deep breath and ask yourself, "What if? What if it's possible? Why not? How could I do that?"

Keep removing disempowering assumptions and replace them with assumptions that give you more freedom and power to change your life and the lives of others. And, more importantly, take action. Move beyond your comfort zone. As you do so, you'll be amazed at the wonderful things you can achieve. Review your empowering assumptions every day and keep refining them until you have a solid web of beliefs that will allow you to design the life you want.

Finally, never stop believing in what's possible. With an unshakable belief in yourself and in your vision, you can do extraordinary things.

If you want to share your story or ask me any questions, please feel free to contact me at: thibaut.meurisse@gmail.com. I always love hearing from my readers.

I wish you all the best,

Thibaut Meurisse

Founder of Whatispersonaldevelopment.org

What do you think?

I want to hear from you! Your thoughts and comments are important to me. If you enjoyed this book or found it useful **I'd be very grateful if you'd post a short review on Amazon.** Your support really does make a difference. I read all the reviews personally so that I can get your feedback and make this book even better.

Thanks again for your support!

OTHER BOOKS BY THE AUTHORS:

Goal Setting: The Ultimate Guide to Achieving Life-Changing Goals (Free Workbook Included)

Habits That Stick: The Ultimate Guide to Building Habits That Stick Once and For All (Free Workbook Included)

Master Your Emotions: A Practical Guide to Overcome Negativity and Better Manage Your Feelings (Free Workbook Included)

Productivity Beast: An Unconventional Guide to Getting Things Done (Free Workbook Included)

The Greatness Manifesto: Overcome Your Fear and Go After What You Really Want

The One Goal: Master the Art of Goal Setting, Win Your Inner Battles, and Achieve Exceptional Results (Free Workbook Included)

The Passion Manifesto: Escape the Rat Race, Uncover Your Passion and Design a Career and Life You Love (Free Workbook Included)

The Thriving Introvert: Embrace the Gift of Introversion and Live the Life You Were Meant to Live (Free Workbook Included)

Upgrade Yourself: Simple Strategies to Transform Your Mindset, Improve Your Habits and Change Your Life

Wake Up Call: How To Take Control Of Your Morning And Transform Your Life (Free Workbook Included)

ABOUT THE AUTHOR

THIBAUT MEURISSE

Thibaut Meurisse is a personal development blogger, author, and founder of whatispersonaldevelopment.org.

He has been featured on major personal development websites such as Lifehack, Goalcast, TinyBuddha, Addicted2Success, MotivationGrid or PickTheBrain.

Obsessed with self-improvement and fascinated by the power of the brain, his personal mission is to help people realize their full potential and reach higher levels of fulfillment and consciousness.

In love with foreign languages, he is French, writes in English, and lived in Japan for almost ten years.

Learn more about Thibaut at:

amazon.com/author/thibautmeurisse

whatispersonaldevelopment.org

thibaut.meurisse@gmail.com

MASTER YOUR EMOTIONS (PREVIEW)

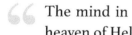 The mind in its own place, and in itself can make a heaven of Hell, a hell of Heaven.

— John Milton, poet.

We all experience a wild range of emotions throughout our lives. I had to admit, while writing this book, I experienced highs and lows myself. At first, I was filled with excitement and thrilled at the idea of providing people with a guide to help them understand their emotions. I imagined how readers' lives would improve as they learned to control their emotions. My motivation was high and I couldn't help but imagine how great the book would be.

Or so I thought.

After the initial excitement, the time came to sit down to write the actual book, and that's when the excitement wore off pretty quickly. Ideas that looked great in my mind suddenly felt dull. My writing seemed boring, and I felt as though I had nothing substantive or valuable to contribute.

Sitting at my desk and writing became more challenging each day. I started losing confidence. Who was I to write a book about emotions if I couldn't even master my own emotions? How ironic! I considered giving up. There are already plenty of books on the topic, so why add one more?

At the same time, I realized this book was a perfect opportunity to work on my own emotional issues. And who doesn't suffer from negative emotions from time to time? We all have highs and lows, don't we? The key is what we *do* with our lows. Are we using our emotions to grow? Are we learning something from them? Or are we beating ourselves up over them?

So, let's talk about *your* emotions now. Let me start by asking you this:

How do you feel right now?

Knowing how you feel is the first step toward taking control of your emotions. You may have spent so much time internalizing you've lost touch with your emotions. Perhaps you answered as follows: "I feel this book could be useful," or "I really feel I could learn something from this book." However, none of these answers reflect how you feel. You don't 'feel like this,' or 'feel like that,' you simply 'feel.' You don't 'feel like' this book could be useful, you 'think' this book could be useful, and that generates an emotion which makes you 'feel' excited about reading it. Feelings manifest as physical sensations in your body, not as an idea in your mind. Perhaps, the reason the word 'feel' is so often overused or misused is because we don't want to talk about our emotions. So, how do you feel now?

Why is it important to talk about emotions?

How you feel determines the quality of your life. Your emotions can make your life miserable or truly magical. That's why they are among the most important things to focus on. Your emotions color all your experiences. When you feel good, everything seems, feels, or tastes better. You also think better thoughts. Your energy levels are higher and possibilities seem limitless. Conversely, when you feel depressed, everything seems dull. You have little energy and you become unmotivated. You feel stuck in a place (mentally and physically) you don't want to be, and the future looks gloomy.

Your emotions can also act as a powerful guide. They can tell you something is wrong and allow you to make changes in your life. As such, they may be among the most powerful personal growth tools you have.

Sadly, neither your teachers nor your parents taught you how emotions work or how to control them. I find it ironic that just about anything comes with a how-to manual, while your mind doesn't. You've never received an instruction manual to teach you how your mind works and how to use it to better manage your emotions, have you? I haven't. In fact, until now, I doubt one even existed.

What you'll learn in this book

This book is the how-to manual your parents should have given you at birth. It's the instruction manual you should have received at school. In it, I'll share everything you need to know about emotions so you can overcome your fears and limitations and become the type of person you really want to be.

You'll learn what emotions are, how they are formed, and how you can use them for your personal growth. You'll also learn how to deal with negative emotions and condition your mind to create more positive emotions.

It is my sincere hope and expectation that, by the end of this book, you will have a clear understanding of what emotions are and will have all the tools you need to start taking control of them.

More specifically, this book will help you:

- Understand what emotions are and how they impact your life
- Identify negative emotions that control your life and learn to overcome them
- Change your story to take better control over your life and create a more compelling future, and
- Reprogram your mind to experience more positive emotions.

Here is a more detailed summary of what you'll learn in this book:

In **Part I**, we'll discuss what emotions are. You'll learn why you are wired to focus on negativity and what you can do to counter this effect. You'll also discover how your beliefs impinge upon your emotions. Finally, you'll learn how negative emotions work and why they are so tricky.

In **Part II**, we'll go over the things that directly impact your emotions. You'll understand the roles your body, your thoughts, your words, or your sleep, play in your life and how you can use them to change your emotions.

In **Part III**, you'll learn how emotions are formed. You'll also learn how to condition your mind to experience more positive emotions.

And finally, in **Part IV**, we'll discuss how to use your emotions as a tool for personal growth. You'll learn why you experience emotions such as fear or depression and how they work. You'll then discover how to use them to grow.

To start mastering your emotions today go to mybook.to/Master_Emotions

I. What emotions are

Have you ever wondered what emotions are and what purpose they serve?

In this section, we'll discuss how your survival mechanism affects your emotions. Then, we'll explain what the 'ego' is and how it impacts your emotions. Finally, we'll discover the mechanism behind emotions and learn why negative emotions can be so hard to deal with.

1. How your survival mechanism affects your emotions

Why people have a bias towards negativity

Your brain is designed for survival, which explains why you're able to read this book at this very moment. When you think about it, the probability of you being born was extremely low. For this miracle to happen, all the generations before you had to survive long enough to procreate. In their quest for survival and procreation, they must have faced death hundreds or perhaps thousands of times.

Fortunately, unlike your ancestors, you're (probably) not facing death every day. In fact, in many parts of the world, life has never been safer. Yet, your survival mechanism hasn't changed much. Your brain still scans your environment looking for potential threats.

In many ways, some parts of your brain have become obsolete. While you may not be seconds away from being eaten by a predator, your brain still gives significantly more weight to negative events than to positive ones.

Fear of rejection is one example of a bias toward negativity. In the past, being rejected from your tribe would reduce your chances of survival significantly. Therefore, you learned to look for any sign of rejection, and this became hardwired in your brain.

Nowadays, being rejected often carries little or no consequence to your long-term survival. You could be hated by the entire world and still have a job, a roof and plenty of food on the table, yet, your brain is still programmed to perceive rejection as a threat to your survival.

This is why rejection can be so painful. While you know most rejections are no big deal, you nevertheless feel the emotional pain. If you listen to your mind, you may even create a whole drama around it. You may believe you aren't worthy of love and dwell on a rejection for days or weeks. Worse still, you may become depressed as a result of this rejection.

In fact, one single criticism can often outweigh hundreds of positive ones. That's why, an author with fifty 5-star reviews, is likely to feel terrible when they receive a single 1-star review. While the author understands the 1-star review isn't a threat to her survival, her authorial brain doesn't. It likely interprets the negative review as a threat to her ego which triggers an emotional reaction.

The fear of rejection can also lead you to over-dramatize events. If your boss criticized you at work, your brain may see the event as a threat and you now think, "What if I'm fired? What if I can't find a job quickly enough and my wife leaves me? What about my kids? What if I can't see them again?" While you are fortunate to have such an effective survival mechanism, it is also your responsibility to separate real threats from imaginary ones. If you don't, you'll experience unnecessary pain and worry that will negatively impact the quality of your life. To overcome this bias towards negativity, you must reprogram your mind. One of a human being's greatest powers is our ability to use our thoughts to shape our reality and interpret events in a more empowering way. This book will teach you how to do this.

Why your brain's job isn't to make you happy

Your brain's primary job is not to make you happy, but to ensure your survival. Thus, if you want to be happy, you must take control of your emotions rather than hoping you'll be happy because it's your natural state. In the following section, we'll discuss what happiness is and how it works.

How dopamine can mess with your happiness

Dopamine is a neurotransmitter which, among other functions, plays a major role in rewarding certain behaviors. When dopamine is released into specific areas of your brain—the pleasure centers—you get a high. This is what happens during exercise, when you gamble, have sex, or eat great food.

One of the roles of dopamine is to ensure you look for food so you don't die of starvation, and you search for a mate so you can reproduce. Without dopamine, our species would likely be extinct by now. It's a pretty good thing, right?

Well, yes and no. In today's world, this reward system is, in many cases, obsolete. While in the past, dopamine was linked to our survival instinct, The release of dopamine can now be generated artificially. A great example of this effect is social media, which uses psychology to suck as much time as possible out of your life. Have you noticed all these notifications that pop up constantly?

They're used to trigger a release of dopamine so you stay connected, and the longer you stay connected, the more money the services make. Watching pornography or gambling also leads to a release a dopamine which can make these activities highly addictive.

Fortunately, we don't need to act each time our brain releases dopamine. For instance, we don't need to constantly check our Facebook newsfeeds just because it gives us a pleasurable shot of dopamine.

Today's society is selling a version of happiness that can make us *un*happy. We've become addicted to dopamine largely because of marketers who have found effective ways to exploit our brains. We receive multiple shots of dopamine throughout the day and we love it. But is that the same thing as happiness?

Worse than that, dopamine can create real addictions with severe consequences on our health. Research conducted at Tulane University showed that, when given permission to self-stimulate their pleasure center, participants did it an average of forty times per minute. They chose the stimulation of their pleasure center over food, even refusing to eat when hungry!

Korean, Lee Seung Seop is an extreme case of this syndrome. In 2005, Mr Seop died after playing a video game for fifty-eight hours straight with very little food or water, and no sleep. The subsequent investigation concluded the cause of death was heart failure induced by exhaustion and dehydration. He was only twenty-eight years old.

To take control of your emotions, it is essential you understand the role dopamine plays and how it affects your happiness. Are you addicted to your phone? Are you glued to your TV? Or maybe you spend too much time playing video games. Most of us are addicted to something. For some people it's obvious, but for others, it's more subtle. For instance, you could be addicted to thinking. To better control your emotions, it is important to shed the light on your addictions as they can rob you of your happiness.

The 'one day I will' myth

Do you believe that one day you will achieve your dream and finally be happy? This is unlikely to happen. You may (and I hope you will) achieve your dream, but you won't live 'happily ever after.' This is just another trick your mind plays on you.

Your mind quickly acclimates to new situations, which is probably the result of evolution and our need to adapt continually in order to survive and reproduce. This is also probably why the new car or house you want will only make you happy for a while. Once the initial excitement wears off, you'll move on to crave the next exciting thing. This phenomenon is known as 'hedonic adaptation.'

How hedonic adaptation works

Let me share an interesting study that will likely change the way you see happiness. This study, which was conducted on lottery winners and paraplegics, was extremely eye-opening for me. Conducted in 1978, the investigation evaluated how winning the lottery or becoming a paraplegic influence happiness:

The study found that one year after the event, both groups were just as happy as they were beforehand. Yes, just as happy (or unhappy). You can find more about it by watching Dan Gilbert's Ted Talk, The Surprising Science of Happiness here.

Perhaps you believe that you'll be happy once you've 'made it.' But, as the above study on happiness shows, this is simply not true. No matter what happens to you, you'll revert back to your predetermined level of happiness once you've adapted to the new event. This is how your mind works.

Does that mean you can't be happier than you are right now? No. What it means is that, in the long run, external events have very little impact upon your level of happiness.

In fact, according to Sonja Lyubomirsky, author of *The How of Happiness*, fifty percent of our happiness is determined by genetics, forty percent by internal factors, and only ten percent by external factors. These external factors include such things as whether we're single or married, rich or poor, and similar social influences.

This suggests, only ten percent of your happiness is linked to external factors, which is probably way less than you thought. The bottom line is this: Your attitude towards life influences your happiness, not what happens to you.

By now, you understand how your survival mechanism impacts negatively your emotions and prevent you from experiencing more joy and happiness in your life. In the next segment/section we'll learn about the ego.

To read more visit my author page at:

amazon.com/author/thibautmeurisse

ACTION GUIDE

Part I. Understanding assumptions

What are your specific assumptions?

Complete the following sentences with whatever comes to your mind. Write as many answers as you like.

- Life is...
- Success is...
- Emotions are...
- I am...
- Money is...
- Time is...
- Work is...

Part II. Uncovering common assumptions

Negative assumption #1 - I'm convinced of something, therefore, it must be true

Exercise: Write down your major assumptions. These are the core beliefs you're most strongly attached to. Start opening yourself up to the possibility they may not be true.

-

-

-

-

-

Negative assumption #2 - My beliefs need to be accurate

Exercise: Select two or three empowering beliefs that would make the biggest difference in your life, if you were to adopt them.

Your assumptions:

-

-

-

Life assumptions

Negative assumption #3 - Life is hard

Exercise: write down all the reasons why your life is easy. Come up with at least twenty reasons. For instance, life is easy because:

- There is food on the table every day
- I have access to water and electricity
- I have great friends I can meet regularly
- I have access to great information online for free or at an affordable price.

-

-

-

-

-

-

-

\-

\-

\-

\-

\-

\-

\-

\-

\-

\-

\-

\-

\-

\-

Negative assumption #4 - Other are happier than me

Exercise: Answer the question: why am I probably as happy as anybody else?

\-

\-

\-

\-

\-

Negative assumption #5 - I'm the product of my environment

Exercise: What could you do to change (and change your environment)? Come up with a couple of simple things you could do to start changing your life.

-

-

Negative assumption #6 - I need to be realistic

Exercise: Answer the following question: in what way are you holding back your potential due to the limitations imposed on you by others?

Negative assumption #7 - If I received more, I would give more

Exercise: What is one thing you could give more of?

Negative assumption #8 - Having problems is a problem

Exercise: Make a list of all your problems. How could you reframe them, so they become less of a problem, or even have them open doors to new opportunities?

Problem #1:

New interpretation:

Problem #2:

New interpretation:

Problem #3:

New interpretation:

Problem #4:

New interpretation:

Problem #5:

New interpretation:

Negative assumption # 9 - Things 'should' be a certain way

Exercise: Make a list of five things you believe should be a certainty but aren't right now. Then, replace "should" by "could". How does it make you feel?

-

-

-

-

-

Negative assumption # 10 - My past equals my future

Exercise: Close your eyes and imagine you could start your day free of any burden from the past. How would it make you feel?

Negative assumption # 11 - I'm not good enough

Exercise: Look at one area in which you tend to blame yourself for not being good enough. Now, say to yourself, "I'm good enough for now." Then, take a step back and put things in perspective. Realize how much room you have to improve and how much time you have to do so. You're good enough *for now*. You can always improve yourself in the future if needed.

Negative assumption #12 - I will believe it when I see it

Exercise: Think of one thing you really want to make happen in the future. Hold the space for it. Make it part of your field of possibilities. Ask yourself:

What if I could create it?

What if it is possible?

Negative assumption #13 - I'm not ready yet

Exercise: Identify one thing you haven't done (yet) because it makes you feel a little uncomfortable. Hold the space for it to happen in the near future.

Could you do it?

Will you?

Negative assumption #14 - If I believe it, I can achieve it

Exercise: Think of one thing you believe is impossible. It could be something you want to ask for or something you want to do. Could you challenge yourself to do it? Will you?

Negative assumption #15 - It's just who I am

Exercise: What disempowering story have you been telling yourself for years? What if the opposite is true? Come up with twenty reasons why this story may not be true.

Your disempowering story:

Why it may not be true:

-

-

-

-

-

-

-

-

-

-

-

-

-

-

-

-

-

-

-

-

Negative assumption #16 - I lack motivation/I'm lazy

Exercise: Look at one area of your life in which you lack motivation. Now, try to identify why that's the case. Is it because you have no interest? Is it because it isn't aligned with your deepest values?

Negative assumption #17 - Self-discipline sucks

Exercise: Imagine if you could do all the things you know you should be doing. How would you feel? What difference would it make to your life? What single habit could help you build self-discipline?

My single habit:

Negative assumption #18 - It's selfish to focus on myself

Exercise: Identify one quality that, if you were to develop, would have a positive impact on people around you. It could be keeping better control over your anger, keeping your promises, becoming a better listener, stopping criticizing people, etc.

One quality I could develop:

Negative assumption #19 - I'm too old

Exercise: Have you ever told yourself you're too old to pursue your goals? If so, identify one goal you talked yourself out of because you considered yourself too old. Go to your favorite search engine and search for 'old' people who have accomplished that same goal. For instance, search 'oldest people' + your goal.

Negative assumption #20 - Telling the truth hurts people and should be avoided

Exercise: If you could tell only one truth you haven't told before. Who would be the person you would tell it to and what would that be?

My one truth:

Assumptions about success

Negative assumption #21 - Success is possible

Exercise: Look at your biggest goal or dream. Now, imagine you were absolutely convinced success was inevitable. How would this make you feel? What action(s) would you take? Spend a couple of minutes playing that scenario in your mind.

Negative assumption #22 - Success is having more

Exercise: Look at the bigger vision you have for yourself. Now, write down all the qualities and skills the future you would embody.

Qualities:

Skills:

Negative assumption #23 - Success is an outcome

Exercise: Based on your current goals, write down your ideal successful day—what you would need to do to feel like a success every day. Select a few simple habits that move you toward this goal. Start with tiny daily goals and achieve them for thirty days. This will help you build more confidence and increase your self-esteem.

Simple habits you could adopt to achieve your goals:

-

-

-

-

Negative assumption #24 - Failure is the opposite of success

Exercise: Clear your mind and connect with your deepest sense of self. Now, realize that none of the 'failures' from your past have ever done anything to you. And no failure will ever. This is a very powerful realization.

Negative assumption #25 - I'm either a success or a failure

Exercise: Select one goal you have failed to achieve. Focus on what you did well. What progress did you make? What did you learn? What could you acknowledge about yourself? Was your intent pure?

Negative assumption #26 - I need to be lucky to be successful

Exercise: Imagine there is no such thing as luck and you are guaranteed to achieve anything you want. What would you do?

Negative assumption #27 - I'm not there yet

Exercise: Imagine there was nowhere else to go, nothing more to do to make you happy and complete. You could just release all the tension for one moment. How would it make you feel?

Negative assumption #28 - I need to achieve big things to feel like I'm a success

Exercise: Who did you help? Make a list of the people you helped in your life. Now, allow yourself to feel good for having help these people.

-

-

-

-

-

Negative assumption #29 - I don't have enough

Exercise: Visualize all the things you ate today. Then, visualize some of your favorite dishes. Realize how blessed you are to have access to such a variety of dishes. Now, visualize yourself in the comfort of your bed. If you wish, you can do this exercise every day in the morning and/or in the evening.

Negative assumption #30 - You can't have it all

Exercise: Visualize what it would look like if you had it all (whatever that means to you). Keep that vision as a possible future. Hold the space for it in your mind.

Negative assumption #31 - I can't ask for what I want

Exercise: Write down the top three things you wanted to ask but didn't. Ask yourself, what if I could ask these things?

Negative assumption #32 - I already know that

Exercise: Write down ten things you believe you know but actually don't, i.e. things you know intellectually but haven't actually applied in your life. The easiest way to do this is to look at results you're after but haven't been able to produce (yet).

-

-

-

-

-

-

-

-

Negative assumption #33 - I've reached a plateau and can't improve anymore

Exercise: Identify an area in which you feel stuck or fail to get the results you want. Ask yourself, what can I do to get unstuck?

Assumptions about money

Negative assumption #34 - Money is not important

Exercise: Answer the following questions with brutal honesty:

If you had enough money to never have to work again, would you still be working at your current job?

Do you often think about money? (Worrying, fantasizing about making more money etc.) What does this say about your relationship with money?

Would you change your life drastically as a result of having more money in your bank account? If so, how?

Now, based on your answers, how important is money to you?

Negative assumption #35 - Money is the root of all evil

Exercise: What is one small action I could take to change my relationship with money and extend my comfort zone? (E.G. give money to charity, invest in myself, charge more for my services, etc.)

My small action:

Negative assumption #36 - Being poor is noble

Exercise: Spend a few seconds to write down the values you give to money, whatever they may be.

Negative assumption #37 - Money is scarce

Exercise: Take a few seconds to meditate on the fact that money isn't something external you need to earn or attract. It comes from within you as one manifestation of wealth.

Negative assumption #38 - Money doesn't grow on trees

Exercise: Write down twenty ways you could attract more money in your life.

-

-

-

-

-

-

-

-

-

-

-

-

-

-

-

-

-

-

Negative assumption #39 - Wealth equals money

Exercise: How resourceful are you? Write down all the qualities and strengths you have and could rely on to attract the resources you need to create wealth. This could be your motivation, passion, creativity, etc.

Assumptions about emotions

Negative assumption #40 - I am my emotions

Exercise: Remember one of the worst things that ever happened to you. Now, notice how it has passed.

Negative assumption #41 - My emotions dictate my actions

Exercise: Knowing you dictate your actions, not your emotions, what will you start doing differently from now? What will you do whether you feel like it or not?

Negative assumption #42 - I get upset because of something external

Exercise: Select something that upset you recently. Look at what happened objectively without adding your interpretation to the event. Notice how the issue probably isn't the event itself, but the story you've attached to it.

Negative assumption #43 - I'm responsible for how other people feel

Exercise: Write down one situation where worrying about how others may feel prevents you from doing something you really want to do.

Negative assumption #44 - Complaining is natural

Exercise: For one full day, refuse to complain about anything. If you want, you can extend this challenge for as long as you like. A great book to read on the topic is Will Bowen's, *A Complaint Free World: How to Stop Complaining and Start Enjoying the Life You Always Wanted.*

Assumptions about work

Negative assumption #45 - I can't find a job I love

Exercise: What does your ideal job look like? Write it down.

Negative assumption #46 - I can't make money doing what I love

Exercise: Write down twenty ideas on how you could make money doing what you love.

-

-

-

-

-

-

-

-

-

-

-

-

-

-

-

-

-

-

-

-

Negative assumption # 47 - I have to work forty plus years and retire at sixty-five

Exercise: Where would you like to be professionally in five years? Write down what your ideal career would look like.

My ideal career:

Negative assumption # 48 - I work hard now so I can enjoy my life once I finally retire

Exercise: answer the following question: Assuming I could never retire and had to work until the day I die, would I still be doing what I'm currently doing?

Assumption about time

Time is one of the most important resources we have. In this section, we'll cover two major assumptions that could prevent you from making the most of your time.

Negative assumption #49 - I don't have enough time

Exercise: For an entire week, write down every activity you do at work and at home. Now, look at all your tasks. Which ones are really productive? Do you really not have time to strive for your goal in life?

Negative assumption #50 - Money is more valuable than time

Exercise: Write down all the tasks you could stop doing because they aren't aligned with your vision or aren't productive.

Part III. Creating new assumptions

Selecting your core life assumptions

Let's start by unearthing your major assumptions about life.

We introduced the following assumptions earlier:

- *Life is easy. And I do whatever I can to keep it this way.*
- *I'm as happy as anybody else.*
- *As I change, my environment changes.*
- *I create my own reality. What others believe I can or cannot do is irrelevant.*
- *By giving more, I open myself to receiving more.*
- *Having problems is normal. The less attached I am to them, the more irrelevant they become.*
- *In any problem lies opportunity.*
- *I fully accept what is, and I can create what will be.*
- *Every day I start anew, free of any burden from the past.*
- *I'm good enough for now.*
- *I'm perfect in my imperfections.*
- *My intent is pure.*
- *I matter.*
- *I believe it, and therefore I'll see it.*
- *Because I start before I'm ready, I can achieve anything I want faster than I ever thought possible.*
- *I ask for whatever I want, regardless of how I feel.*
- *I'm the scriptwriter of my life, and I can rewrite my story at will.*
- *I'm motivated because I have a motive for action.*
- *Self-discipline equals freedom. With enough self-discipline, I can achieve anything I want.*
- *I take care of me for my family and friends.*

- *I'm never too old to do what I want to do*
- *I help others and myself grow by telling the truth whenever possible.*

To begin with select only five assumptions in this list. If you were to adopt them, what five assumptions would make the biggest difference in your life?

-

-

-

-

-

Selecting assumptions in major areas of your life

Now you have selected your top five life assumptions, let's look at some major assumptions you could adopt in various areas of your life.

Below is a summary of the assumptions we introduced previously:

Success

- *Success is inevitable.*
- *Success is not about what I have, it's about who I become.*
- *I happily fail my way to success. I fail faster and better each time.*
- *I'm successful because I'm making progress toward my goal.*
- *I create my own success regardless of external circumstances.*
- *I'm already there, and I'm more than enough for now.*
- *By having changed some people's lives, even in a minor way, I'm already a huge success.*

- *I have good intentions, therefore I'm a massive success.*
- *Food + shelter = happiness + success*
- *I can have it all.*
- *I allow myself to ask for what I want.*
- *If I don't live it, I don't know it.*
- *Everything is learnable, and I can always improve.*

Money

- *Money is important.*
- *I give myself total permission to give and receive money in abundance.*
- *The more money I have, the more people I can help.*
- *Wealth is unlimited, and I can always create more of it.*
- *Wealth creation is inevitable, I just have to plant the right seeds.*
- *I'm the source of wealth. I have enough resourcefulness to attract any resources I need to create wealth.*

Emotions

- *Emotions come and go. What I am, remains untouched. Forever.*
- *I dictate my actions, regardless of the way I feel.*
- *Nothing outside of me has the power to upset me.*
- *I'm responsible for how I feel, not for how other people feel.*
- *I refuse to complain. I do something about it or I accept it.*

Work

- *I can find a job I love, and I will!*
- *I can absolutely make money doing what I love.*
- *I have the power to design my career the way I want to.*
- *I proactively design a career I love and enjoy my life now.*

Time

- *I make the time to do whatever I'm committed to doing.*
- *I value my time because I value myself.*

Now, let's see how you can start creating a new identity by using some of these empowering assumptions.

Creating your Identity Map

Create branches for each area in which you want to implement new empowering assumptions. Remember, this is all about *you* and the life you want to create for *yourself*. Start with the questions: Who do I want to become? If I were to adopt them, what new empowering assumptions would allow me to be that person?

Creating reminders

Now you have your Identity Map, put it somewhere you can see it every day. I recommend you put it on your wall, on your desk and/or in a notebook you carry with you.

Your 30-Day Challenge

Dedicate the next thirty days to implementing new and empowering assumptions. Go through the process summarized below.

Step-by-step method to creating your new identity

1. Create an *Identity Map*

- Select your core life assumptions.
- Select assumptions in each area of your life.

2. **Repeat your assumptions each day** for at least ten minutes, (five minutes in the morning, five minutes in the evening). Follow the process below:

- Repeat your assumptions, (in your mind or out loud),
- Ask yourself why it is true.
- Energize your assumptions by engaging your emotions.
- Envision the concrete actions you can take.

3. **Check how you feel.** If you feel resistance, work through it.

- Identify where you feel the emotion in your body.
- Stay present with it until it starts dissolving. Focus on the most intense part of the emotion.

- Repeat this process as many times as necessary for the fear to dissipate.

4. Create reminders

- Put your mind map on your wall, desk and/or in a notebook you carry with you.
- Write down your assumptions on flashcards and review them several times each day.

Asking "What if?"

An effective way to stretch yourself beyond your comfort zone is to look at each of the following areas of your life and ask yourself, *"What if?"*

- Career
- Family/friends
- Finance
- Health/fitness
- Relationship
- Personal growth

Answer the following questions.

Career

What if I could have the perfect career?

Family/friends

What if I could experience and share more joy than I ever have with my family and friends?

Finance

What if I could double my income by the end of the year?

Health/fitness

What if I could have lots of energy and feel great every day?

Personal growth

What if I could overcome my fears and grow beyond my imagination?

Relationship

What if I could take my relationship to a whole new level?

Visualize what your life would look like in each of the above situations.

Going beyond your realm of possibility

Stretch yourself further by answering the following questions. Feel free to come up with your own questions.

Career

What if I could have the perfect career in exactly the way I want it?

What if I could change my career within twelve months? Six months? One month?

What if I could change my career this week?

Family/friends

What if I could experience ridiculous levels of bliss and joy in presence of my family and friends? What if I could feel total gratitude for every person who ever showed up in my life?

Finance

What if I could double my income within a year? Within six months? Within thirty days?

What if I could generate ten times my income within a year?

Health/fitness

What if the level of joy I've experienced so far is just a fraction of the level my real self can experience?

What if I could experience intense feelings of bliss as never before?

Personal growth

What if I'm currently just a tiny fraction of the person I could be?

What if I'm just scratching the surface of what is possible for me in this world?

What if I could remove any fear, self-about and limitations in any area of my life and move freely in this world?

Relationship

What if I could take my relationship to a whole new level and one I didn't even know exist?

Committing to the impossible

Let's take this exercise one step further. For each area, ask yourself, "If I had to achieve this crazy vision, what would I do?"

Play along and imagine you had to achieve your goals at all cost. Force yourself to think in a way you've never thought before.

Made in United States
North Haven, CT
01 March 2023

33391140R00108